THE END
OF
DEMOCRACY

THE END
OF
DEMOCRACY

by

Christophe Buffin de Chosal

Translated by:
Ryan P. Plummer

TUMBLAR HOUSE
Bona Tempora Volvant

Arcadia
MMXVII

Printed in the United States of America

ISBN 978-1-944339-08-1

The End of Democracy
Copyright © 2014 by Christophe Buffin de Chosal.

Originally published in France in 2014 as
La Fin de la Démocratie.

English translation
Copyright © 2017 by Ryan P. Plummer

Published by Tumblar House
Visit our website at www.tumblarhouse.com

"Sometime in the coming century, people will rack their brains pondering how nations with tremendous scientific and intellectual achievements could have given uninstructed and untrained men and women the right to vote equally uninstructed and untrained people into responsible positions."

- Erik von Kuehnelt-Leddihn

TABLE OF CONTENTS

FOREWORD

Charles A. Coulombe

THIS book may well be one of the most important you have ever read—at least in terms of politics. Christophe Buffin de Chosal makes his intention quite clear in his own Introduction:

> ...what you are going to read presents at each moment the two facets of democracy: the delusion and the deception. The delusion consists in believing that a political system which is unrealistic, artificial, and directly at odds with human nature could contribute to mankind's happiness. Because it claimed to be rooted in lofty principles, the democratic ideal had to be true and good, regardless of any rational observation to the contrary. This delusion has accompanied all democratic and democratically derived systems up to the present day.
>
> Then, there is the deception, because this delusion has veiled the fraud and sordid machinations of those who have exploited democracy to serve their particular interests. The two elements are inseparable and have been found side by side from the beginning of democratic ideas up until democracy's everyday practice in our own time.

He concisely answers the obvious objection:

> A democrat who is driven into a corner (which happens very quickly since no one is prepared to defend what is reputed as unassailable) easily says, "What do

1

you then propose instead?" This is the trap one must not
fall into. It is necessary first to question the principles
and expose the deviating praxis in what one today calls
"democracy."

As he rightly tells us, we cannot begin to think of
something better until we admit the evils of what we
have. Here an admission is in order; my own *Star-
Spangled Crown* was inspired partly by the questions
raised in reading the French edition of this book.

As he makes crystal clear, Buffin de Chosal has
not come to save democracy, but to bury it. This he
does in the following chapters in a devastating manner.
Mercilessly, both in terms of logical argumentation
and factual citation, he dissects the dominant political
mythos of our day. Layer by layer he peels back the
lies to reveal the terrible truth: this particular Emperor
really does have no clothes, and the "democratic
system" that dominates the West serves merely to veil
the operations of an oligarchy. What makes his
message all the more timely and important is that—as
with the refugee issue in Europe and the transgendered
military conflict in this country—it is an oligarchy
ever more removed from reality, and ideologically
committed to a course that can end only in world-wide
ruin and misery.

It will, however, be noted that many of the points
in Buffin de Chosal's analysis relate to the countries
of Europe or the European Union. It has certainly been
a commonplace of American "Conservatism" that
American democracy, like American Liberalism,
differs not in degree but in kind from the Continental
variety. This idea has received support from such truly
eminent men as Russell Kirk, who was at great pains

to distinguish the "good" American Revolution from the "bad" French Revolution. It received universal expression in the Catholic world through the influence of Fr. John Courtney Murray, S.J. at Vatican II—and received apparent real world confirmation through the spectacle of Eisenhower's America protecting the Free World from Communism.

That, however, was over a half century ago, and in the wake of both the 1960s and the aftermath of the fall of the Soviet Bloc, the apparent differences between the European and American versions have vanished, leaving a Transatlantic Oligarchical consensus that attempts to strangle any semblance of past morality and tradition. That our own revolution and subsequent history were different in kind from the French and other such European/Latin American conflicts have been increasingly challenged—not only by foreign scholars such as the Canadians George Grant and Ron Dart and the Argentine Antonio Caponnetto, but by American historians of widely varying ideologies, such as Kevin Phillips, Gordon S. Wood, Thomas B. Allen, Eric Nelson, Thomas McConville, and a seemingly endless and ever expanding list of others. In a word, the American exceptionalism that is a dogma among many on what we think of as the American Right is not merely being disproved by everyday experience of the present, but increasingly by unsparing examination of the past.

With that in mind, it is important to read this book without making the mental reservations that so many of us are prone to do when reading the writings of European or Latin American Conservatives: "Well, that may be true of Italy or Peru, but it is different here!" On the contrary, it is true in France, in these United States, in Chile, in Australia, and wherever it is pretended that the "people" rule. Reality is the same everywhere, and living under the Star-Spangled Banner gives us no immunity to it. If you read *The End of Democracy* without red, white, and blue coloured glasses, you will learn much—starting, perhaps, with the European Union's uncanny resemblance to our Federal Government. If you want to know how as much governmentally-mandated societal change as we have seen in the past decades can occur without popular approval, look no further. This book is for you.

A note must be made about the author. Christophe Buffin de Chosal comes of a distinguished Belgian noble family on the one hand, and is Professor of Economic History at the United Business Institutes on the other. That is to say that he has one foot firmly planted in the world of history and tradition, and the other in the modernity of business and economics—it is this unique combination of perspectives that allows him to see what many others do not. He is also a devout Catholic; in 2012, he authored a book in French entitled *Les vraies raisons pour lesquelles les églises se vident*— "The Real Reasons Churches Empty Themselves." In examining the actual reasons for Catholicism's contemporary decline, he brings the same gimlet eye he exhibits in this volume.

It must be confessed that he offers—as he threatened he would not—no direct alternative. The book ends on a doleful—almost apocalyptic—note. But in the Faith that once built Christendom, and the natural human qualities of authority, solidarity, and loyalty that accompanied that building, he sees hope. For Buffin de Chosal is quite right: we cannot begin to see solutions until we admit we have a problem—those solutions inevitably shall include the three things that the Modern World has been in revolt against since the 16th century: altar, throne, and hearth.

Charles A. Coulombe
Monrovia, California
August 6, 2017
Feast of the Transfiguration

INTRODUCTION

DEMOCRACY is not just a political system. It is much more, and its nature approaches that of the gods if we consider with how much respect it is treated and with what devotion it is honored. The idolatrous character of democracy is clearly seen in the absolute refusal to question it in any way. Since the end of the last world war, the Western mentality has been as though traumatized by the experience of totalitarian and dictatorial regimes, in the face of which democracy has been presented as the unique means of safeguarding civilization and human dignity. Fundamental political criticism, the kind that questions political systems and their principles, is not applied to democracy, which is held as an essential good without which nothing is certain but chaos, oppression, and misery.

Today no one is disturbed to hear about the United States wanting to institute democracy in the countries of the world where it intervenes militarily. We smile perhaps at the pretext, but not at the principle. We do not think twice about the incongruity of the matter since democracy is seen as the political system of man. It is presented as an unshakable truth or an irreversible acquisition of humanity. It is synonymous with progress. It passes as necessary and beneficial in all cultures and all parts of the world. It would be the universal political system, the final outcome of mankind's long political journey. Because of this, it escapes all questioning and its foundations appear infallibly true.

Is this not to forget that democracy is, after all, only a human invention? It is the fruit of philosophical thought and the result of historical circumstances. It therefore carries a certain risk of error. We can live in the conviction that humanity progresses unceasingly and that what is more recent is likely better than what was before—a conviction on which the contemporary mindset is largely based—but we should still not forget that every human invention is fallible and thus liable to criticism. To hold the contrary is foolish or pretentious.

Besides, it is contrary to progress. Progress can only exist when we are convinced we can do better and that things can be perfected. How is it, then, we became convinced we could do no better than democracy?

It is therefore not only permissible but also necessary to critique democracy. True democrats, if they are to be found, cannot be offended by this because they themselves champion freedom of expression as a fundamental right. True democrats bow before the majority opinion, not because it is true, but for the sole reason that it has the backing of numbers. Because of this, they should refrain from rejecting any opinion as being false, immoral, or scandalous. They should regard any opinion, even a minority one, as a potentially acceptable opinion, an opinion only needing the support of the masses to be accepted and respected. Such an attitude would be consistent with the principles of democracy.

But true democrats are quite rare. There exist in democracy opinions for which you incur definitive censure. There are even some for which you are thrown into prison. Democracy, like any other system, fights tooth and nail to defend its foundations. It mercilessly crushes those who threaten it, and declares, with the coolest self-assurance, that it is on the side of good.

To challenge such a conviction requires a serious argument which, as a lever, can shake and then topple over the bulk of the edifice. A perhaps overblown confidence in human reason enables us to think that when principles are shown to be false, that it is easy for any honest observer to detach himself from them and to take up again the search for truth. For what should we expect of erroneous principles, if not a deviating praxis? All of this would be very easy, of course, if democracy was only a political system. In its particular case, however, we come up against a considerable dose of the irrational. It is placed above reason. Its truthfulness stands outside of any proof or demonstration. It is reputed to be true, independently of reason, and what is more serious, independently of human nature.

With that being said, the objective of this work is simply to confront democracy, its principles and its practice, with the demands of good sense, justice, and nature. It is a modest objective. It is not a question here of elaborating on a new political system—even if we are able to make out the contours of it through the critique of democracy—for such an aim is very unwise and makes one particularly vulnerable. A democrat who is driven into a corner (which happens very quickly since no one is prepared to defend what is reputed as unassailable) easily says, "What do you then propose instead?"

This is the trap one must not fall into. It is necessary first to question the principles and expose the deviating praxis in what one today calls "democracy." It is necessary first, through a detached and rational examination of democracy's vices, to work up to the conclusion that a better system is certainly possible. This patient and methodical approach does not allow the smugness of the opponent to intimidate. Challenging democracy, a system universally practiced, defended, and honored, is a risky undertaking most of our contemporaries will consider utter foolishness and the beginning of lunacy.

Yet it is precisely the foolishness and lunacy of the democratic system that must be exposed. The critique of democracy is an act of confidence in man's rational nature. It is to uncover the delusion and deception of which humanity—the Western world in particular— has been the victim since the time of the French Revolution and even earlier.

Thus, what you are going to read presents at each moment the two facets of democracy: the delusion and the deception. The delusion consists in believing that a political system which is unrealistic, artificial, and directly at odds with human nature could contribute to mankind's happiness. Because it claimed to be rooted in lofty principles, the democratic ideal had to be true and good, regardless of any rational observation to the contrary. This delusion has accompanied all democratic and democratically derived systems up to the present day.

Then, there is the deception, because this delusion has veiled the fraud and sordid machinations of those who have exploited democracy to serve their particular interests. The two elements are inseparable and have been found side by side from the beginning of democratic ideas up until democracy's everyday practice in our own time.

To speak of the end of democracy does not therefore have as an objective, as one might expect, to worry and alert consciences in order to try at all costs to save it. Democracy has been a system in perpetual degradation. It has participated in the decline of the Western world, being both its cause and its fellow traveler. It is a factor of "decivilization," and it leaves in its wake disappointed and politically immature peoples. Behind the screen of its rituals, it consolidates oligarchic totalitarian regimes which shall one day surprise—indeed, this day has already come—peoples who believed themselves free.

Chapter 1

THE "SELF-RULING" PEOPLE

W E often hear it said that "in a democracy, it is the people who rule." This quality of the political system is presented as decisive, as a complete reversal of political doctrine with regard to the divine right of kings. In reality, it is nothing of the sort. Rule by the people is a myth which loses all substance once confronted with the real practice in democracy.

Democracy is not, in its origin, a system of the people. In England with the advent of the parliamentary system just as in France during the Revolution, it was not the people who were seen at work. Even the Russian Revolution was not a phenomenon of the people. To regard the people or what the communists elegantly call the "masses" as the agent of change or political upheaval is purely a theoretical view, a historical myth, of which one sees no trace in reality. The "people" were the pretext, the dupes, and almost always the victims of the revolutions, not the engines.

The French Revolution was built on the idea of the "nation," which claimed to bring together the intellectual, social, and financial elite of the country. It was on this foundation that democracy was established and that it functioned during almost all of the nineteenth century. This "nation" met the desires of the philosophers who wanted to transfer power from the monarch to an enlightened, philosophical, and philanthropic class who, moreover, ought to be financially comfortable. The educated bourgeoisie of the time were the protagonists of this idea, and a portion of the nobility formed their audience. Voltaire wanted to reserve the exercise of power to this superior class. He went so far as to say that the common people should not be taught to read for fear they might vie with the elite for power.

This idea of Voltaire's was inspired by what he had learned of parliamentary monarchy in England. He had seen, rightly so, a class system where the king, under the law, that is to say under Parliament, could no longer act freely in defense of the national interest or that of the more ordinary people, particularly the peasantry.

The appearance of the parliamentary system in England was tied to the great movement of Church property confiscation begun under Henry VIII and continuing until the coming of the Stuarts.[1] When Henry ordered an inventory of the Church's property and then its confiscation at the profit of the crown, he had in mind the dual objective of enrichment and popularity. He sought in effect to win the loyalty of new and old nobility who still regarded the Tudors as a weakly founded dynasty whose right to rule was questionable. Henry VIII generously distributed goods which did not belong to him: revenues from bishoprics, parishes, hospitals, and all kinds of charitable and academic institutions dependent upon

---

[1] Worth reading are the historical works of Hilaire Belloc on the ties in England between the Reformation, parliamentarianism, and capitalism.

the Church and whose financing was exclusively private. Most especially, he distributed stolen lands of abbeys whose monks he had driven out.

He thereby set off a general movement of pillaging which ultimately went beyond the crown's control and took place over the course of centuries. The crown itself did not succeed in keeping all the benefits of the confiscations. It soon found itself surrounded and taken hostage by a recently enriched aristocracy more powerful than itself.

This diminishing of royal power in England was largely assisted by the circumstances: for a century, the crown was placed on precarious heads. Henry VIII's son, Edward VI, was a child when he ascended to the throne, and he died at sixteen years of age. He reigned under the influence of his uncles. His half-sister Mary was Catholic, while her close entourage had good reasons not to be, being tied to recently acquired wealth. Elizabeth, Henry VIII's illegitimate daughter, owed staying in power to her flexibility vis-à-vis this enriched class, which assisted her and, when needed, constrained her in the exercise of government. When Elizabeth died, there was James I, who was a Scot, that is to say a foreigner with respect to the English, and his power was thereby lessened. His son, Charles I, was the first English sovereign to ascend to the throne without handicap since the death of Henry VIII in 1547. He was a male monarch, quite legitimate, Protestant, and English. He undertook to restore royal power after eighty years of weakness during which a wealthy and powerful class had taken shape. He clashed with them and was beheaded.

This glimpse into English history would not make sense without taking into account the Protestant Reformation. Henry VIII, although he broke with Rome and robbed the Catholic Church in his country, still maintained Catholic liturgical rites and general doctrine. But his son, Edward VI, pressed by his entourage, introduced the Reformation in England, for Protestantism afforded a justification for the pillaging of the Church's goods, past and future. No Catholic in good conscience could seize Church property and keep it permanently. Sooner or later he would find himself in an untenable moral situation that the Reformation, inimical to the Church and its goods, happened to conveniently resolve. All those who adopted the Reformation were thus justified in possessing the Church's goods and even in increasing their patrimony at its expense. In so doing, they were fighting "idolatry."

We must not conclude that all Catholics who adopted the Reformation were motivated by prospects of material gain. But it would be naive to think these prospects were not a decisive factor in a great number of conversions and, very likely, the majority of them among the nobility and bourgeoisie. England adopted the Reformation under the impulsion of a minority motivated by profit. For these persons, religion served as a pretext.

The families who had thus helped themselves to the Church's goods, morally justified by Protestant ethics, formed the gentry, the class of landowners who sat in Parliament. Parliament was not then, as one might believe today, an organ of popular representation. It was an instrument in the hands of the gentry to defend its own class interests. It would take too long to detail here the mechanisms which enabled this wealthy class to so formidably build up its power that it would eventually challenge the king. One need only remember this: Parliament, which voted on the crown's budget, had attained a stranglehold on the monarchy, and the latter had fallen by insisting on its rights. At the center of the disagreement between Charles I and the members of Parliament was the property of the Church, confiscated at the profit of the crown long ago and wrongfully held by certain members of the gentry. Charles I wanted restitution. He was unable to match the opposition of the Protestant financial elite, who found in Cromwell a staunch and merciless defender, all the more so because his personal interests were directly threatened by the king's demands.[2]

The financial incentives for England's adoption of the Protestant Reformation are therefore intimately connected with the bolstering of parliamentary power. The Parliament in England was used to put the monarchy in check and to replace it with an oligarchic class of wealthy Protestants to whom the kings were required to submit. This is why the overthrow of James II in 1688 was a true revolution. It was not a popular revolution or the overthrowing of a tyranny, but it was the rebellion of a class implementing the transfer of sovereign power for its own profit.

The French Revolution followed a similar pattern. It did not bear the marks of a unanimous popular

---

[2] Oliver Cromwell owed his considerable fortune to Thomas Cromwell, his great-great-uncle, who carried out the confiscations in the name of Henry VIII, and generously helped himself in the process.

movement. It was principally members of the bourgeoisie and some aristocrats who initiated it at the meeting of the Estates-General. The works of Augustin Cochin[3] aim to demonstrate that the revolutionary intention was already present in the selection of delegates to the Estates-General. The most informed observers of the time[4] portrayed the French Revolution as a conspiracy. Even if it escaped the control of those who instigated it, the Revolution never took on a popular form. It remained a bourgeois phenomenon, replacing the power derived from birth with that derived from money. It instituted censitary suffrage,[5] which remained the dominant form of suffrage into the nineteenth century. It abolished the privileges of the guilds in order to give free range to the capitalists. It abolished the privileges of the peasantry in order to give the industrialists cheap labor.

The parliamentary regimes which issued from the French Revolution imitated the British system: a king not in charge, ministers responsible to the Houses, and, above all, no universal suffrage. The bourgeois regimes' distrust of universal suffrage is easily understood. At the time, universal suffrage would have reinforced the conservatives, for the population would have spontaneously voted for its natural elite: manorial

---

[3] See, for example, Augustin Cochin, *La crise de l'histoire révolutionnaire: Taine et M. Aulard*, 2nd ed. (Paris: Librairie Ancienne Honoré Champion, 1909).

[4] Abbé [Augustin] Barruel, *Mémoires pour servir à l'histoire du jacobinisme* (Hamburg: P. Fauche, 1798-1799).

[5] Censitary suffrage was a restrictive form of suffrage whereby only those wealthy enough to pay the cens, a designated minimum tax threshold, enjoyed the right to vote.—Trans.

lords, notaries, and parish priests. The liberals, who constituted only a small minority of the population, would have lost their political power. Towards the end of the nineteenth century, the two states practicing universal suffrage were also the two most powerful and most conservative monarchies: Germany and Austria-Hungary.

Censitary suffrage ensured power stayed in the hands of a wealthy minority. One could vote if he owned land or factories. Less than ten percent of the population enjoyed the right to vote—less than in Athens at the time of Pericles. It was lawful for the individual, of course, to become wealthy and acquire the right to vote by paying the cens.[6] Theoretically, the electoral class was open, but in practice the wealthy had very well decided not to share with those who were not, and whose vote would have considerably changed the majority.

The bourgeois parliamentary system, which was that of the European democracies of the nineteenth century, was inspired by the English system in which the Bill of Rights made Parliament the true ruler. Never, in the spirit of this system, was sovereignty to fall into the hands of all the people. The parliamentarians had thus obtained power to make laws which served their own interests, first those of the gentry, and then those of the industrial and commercial bourgeoisie. The true purpose of Parliament was to subjugate the monarchy in order to obtain sovereignty and exercise power for its own ends.

---

[6] See note 5 above.

One spoke of "popular rule" because it would have been difficult to admit to the principle of a "bourgeois rule," but under this generous appellation it was the power of one class which was imposed and consolidated. "Universal suffrage will never happen," Minister Guizot said. The people of this period, moreover, would have considered it utter madness to grant the right to vote to the unlearned and illiterate, and believed it necessary to have a minimum amount of education to vote. It was thought then that someone well-informed voted well. It is true that, at the time, the means of mass communication did not belong to the state, nor were they subsidized by it.

Just as in the case of the English Revolution, the French Revolution was nothing other than a successful ploy to take power out of the impartial hands of the king in order to place it into the hands of the rich. The pretext of fighting for freedom, invoked in both cases, was only a deceptive cover. Liberal democracy did not want liberty for all, but only the liberty of the wealthy. If this was not true, how does one explain the prohibition against strikes and unions in the name of economic liberty, and the revocation of legislative power by way of censitary suffrage?

In any case, the term "democracy" does not exactly correspond to this bourgeois parliamentarianism in existence prior to universal suffrage. Does the term not better correspond to the system defined by the principle of "one man, one vote"? The passage of time can make one think the parliamentary systems of the nineteenth century were systems of transition which could only evolve towards universal suffrage. A teleological view of history, whose naiveté is more and more evident, presents contemporary democracy as a resolution of parliamentary tensions of the preceding centuries. The democratic system is therefore considered final. Even if its practice still leaves something to be desired, its principles are reputed to be absolutely true.

The transfer of sovereignty to the people as a whole did not, however, give more surety to the people or to its sovereignty. Much importance is given these days, it seems, to the will of the majority and to the consent of the people, but at the same time there are record rates of abstention in the elections. A hundred years ago democrats fought to obtain universal suffrage. They saw themselves as trailblazers and envisioned the gratitude of future generations of voters happy to exercise their power of self-rule. How disappointed they would be to see that a third of the electorate today relinquishes their right to vote!

A democracy with such a high rate of abstention is certainly an unhealthy system. One might view this as a temporary crisis. One might also understand that democracy is an impossible system.

Popular sovereignty is first of all a contradiction in terms. It is impossible for the people to exercise sovereignty, for they are inevitably divided amongst themselves in their race for power. Unity is a characteristic inseparable from sovereignty. To transfer sovereignty to the people is to condemn it to such a fragmentation that it loses all reality. Democratic society is not only divided according to orientations, ideologies and political factions, but it is also an individualistic society. It is not an organic society in the sense that the Ancien Régime was with its corps and privileged orders. It is atomized and unorganized. The people in it do not represent a whole which is capable of embodying sovereignty, but a multitude of disparate, even conflicting, elements. Even if they were validly represented by political parties, the people would be incapable of exercising sovereignty through the mediation of groups who oppose each other and vie for power.

Since democracy's beginnings, there has been a monumental error concerning the true identity of the people. This may seem paradoxical since democracy is supposed to be the system of the people par excellence. Few systems, none to be exact, claim to represent the people, its welfare, its rights and its sovereignty more than democracy. And yet democracy seems to be unaware of who the people truly are. Actually, it is very well aware. The great democrats know quite well who the people are, but they distrust them. Nothing is more dangerous to democracy than the people. That is why democracy will always claim to serve the people while only permitting a small number to rule in their stead. What democracy demands from the people is legitimacy. It does not care about their opinion.

In the Ancien Régime, the people were not sovereign, nor did they claim to be so. Sovereignty was embodied in the monarch, who ruled and governed. The monarch was a true sovereign insofar as he was not divided against himself or enmeshed in quarrels of interest. He was *superanus*, sovereign, that is to say above organized society and therefore free in his decisions. Still, the people were not absent. The people were represented in the estates, representative bodies convoked by province or generality, and which were found in various forms throughout all of Europe.

The estates neither were nor wanted to be democratic representative bodies. They did not represent individuals but interests tied to orders (clergy, nobility, bourgeoisie and peasantry). The entire organic structure of the Ancien Régime rested not on the individual, but on corps and orders, endowed with privileges and powers to defend their proper interests. This was one of the counterbalances to the monarchy. The monarchy without the corps and orders became a tyranny; the corps and orders without the monarchy begot chaos, civil war, and soon the tyranny of an oligarchy or single man.

The realism of the Ancien Régime lay in the fact that the people were not expected to govern or even to advise the government. They were expected, in an organized way, to represent their interests. The people were certainly not consulted except in these things. But at least, concerning their interests, they did not say anything senseless, for they were speaking of what they knew best. The guilds were consulted about their professional interests and the clergy about their interests tied to religion and works of charity. The Estates-General of 1614—the last convoked in France before 1789—is very illustrative of how interests were defended. It was at this time the bourgeoisie demanded they only continue to pay tallage on the condition that the nobility remain restricted from entering into the professions.[7]

---

[7] See Frantz Funck-Brentano, *L'Ancien Régime* (Paris: Librairie Arthème Fayard, 1942); François Bluche, *L'Ancien Régime: Institutions et société* (Paris: Éditions de Fallois, 1993).

Faced with these disparate interests, often complementary and at times conflicting, all the freedom and power of the monarchy was necessary in order to maintain the peace and the cohesion of the social body. A weak monarchy, as in England, would be subjugated to the interests of a more powerful class to the detriment of other classes' interests. A strong monarchy could, after having listened to all parties, impose the decision which best served the common good, even against certain particular interests. Such a monarchy played the role of the arbiter among factions, a role that does not exist in democracy because its government is itself derived from factions.

The concept of an organic society was abolished at the time of the French Revolution. The corps and orders were suppressed, the privileges were abolished, and everything which allowed the people to protect themselves from the power of the state was banished in the name of liberty. What were the people given in exchange? Sovereignty. They were given the false promise that they would no longer need to defend themselves from the state since they themselves were the state. But if a people organized into corps and orders are incapable of exercising sovereignty, how much more so a people comprising a formless mass of individuals!

This incapacity of the democratic people was intended and planned. A people incapable of exercising power over themselves are condemned to entrust their fate to their representatives, the political parties, who will thenceforth be the true sovereigns. They will exercise the power, legitimized by elections, over an unorganized people without natural defenses to face the power of the state.

This is how the people are regarded in a democracy: a formless and unorganized mass of indistinct individuals. They are like dough in the hands of the state. This people are deprived of organization in the face of the state. The sole organs of resistance which can raise their heads to the state are the political parties and unions—themselves politicized, that is to say under control. The people are condemned to have themselves represented by organizations which are designated to them and outside of which no legal representation is possible. They believe—because they have been told so—that the electoral process is the best way to have themselves represented, while in reality the purpose of the electoral system is not to represent the population but to ensure the elite have power that is regarded as legitimate.

It is thanks to this legitimacy that democratic power enjoys a stranglehold on the people that is without precedence in the history of governmental systems. The supposedly free democratic people are given laws and taxed, without consultation, at the initiative of parties who sit in their name. The democratic people are instructed in schools that the state controls, subsidizes and regulates. They are informed by media the state owns or controls by means of regulations, subsidies, or groups of influence. They take medications the state authorizes, and they eat food the state stamps. The money they use is under the control of the state, which fixes its value and interest rate. The list of the state's prerogatives is long, and it can only justify them through elections.

In the Ancien Régime these prerogatives did not exist. We can ask ourselves with good reason which of the two peoples, that of the Ancien Régime's traditional monarchy or that of the parliamentary democracy, is freer. There, where the democratic people can boast of an entirely theoretical freedom that evaporates in the fire of the state's systematic interventionism, the Ancien Régime was for its part "bristling with freedoms," to borrow the expression of Charles Maurras, freedoms that were very practical and associated with specific purposes, despite the power of the monarchy.

It would be naive to believe that a lever of power such as the democratic state, which legislates, taxes, instructs, informs, physically cares for, feeds, and so forth, a non-resisting population, would be quietly left in the hands of those elected by the people, at the mercy of their caprices and of electoral chance. The political parties secured their power quite some time ago in order to evade this risk which the people represent. But this power evades even them, for they themselves are the playthings of those more powerful than they.

The people in a democracy are the object of all kinds of manipulations and deceptions. They were taken from the land by massive industrialization, instructed by compulsory education, and then informed by television. They believed this to be an effect of their liberation and social ascendancy. In order that they are oblivious to the chains which bind them, the people are filled to excess by a society of consumerism, are overwhelmed by advertising, and their will is eroded by hedonistic pleasures. They get over paying taxes by treating themselves to vacations. The ruling powers encourage them to do so, for inasmuch as they work and enjoy themselves, inasmuch as they pay taxes and consume, they are not involved in politics and they do their part to keep the system going.

Because they are individualistic, the democratic people are not organized. They are incapable of taking a stand. They sense themselves powerless in the face of the state, and indeed they are. This atomization is aggravated today by the mass immigration which the countries of Europe are experiencing, and which is desired by the states and the European Union. The sense of belonging and popular identity dissipates amidst the fragmentation into ethnic communities, ghettos and lawless areas, and even through interracial blending. Immigration inhibits national characteristics and renders society yet more passive and yet more able to be manipulated by the state.

Terms such as "population," "public opinion," "civil society," and "international community" tend to make one think of real interlocutors and aim to give a kind of legitimacy to the ruling powers. But the population is not expressing itself, and when it does by way of referendum or petition, it is not heeded. The Irish referendum on the Treaty of Lisbon proved to be nothing but a sinister farce. Public opinion is a creation of the media, of the ruling powers in other words. And if it is contrary to what the powers want, it is denied. As for the "international community," that is simply some of the world's powerful people gathered around a table, who are themselves subject to yet more powerful lobbies.

Therefore, the best definition of democracy is not "government of the people" or "rule by the people," for these expressions are utopian and meant to deceive. The best definition was given by the Russian philosopher Vasily Rozanov (d. 1919): "Democracy is the system by which an organized minority governs an unorganized majority." This "unorganized majority" is the people, aggregated and individualistic, incapable of reaction because disjointed.

This definition of democracy is consistent with the notion of "utilitarian enframing"[8] Yvan Blot brought to light.[9] The individual therein is considered as human material—"the most important of raw materials"—able to be exchanged or manipulated at will. He is reduced solely to his utilitarian aspects of producer, consumer, and taxpayer. He is merely a tool programmed by the media and education, and distracted from his natural aspirations by occupational work (necessary to assure his subsistence and to repay his debts), leisure activities, and the material and sensual pleasures to which he looks forward. This schema contrived for the totalitarian regimes of the twentieth century suits even better the democratic societies of the twenty-first century, which have followed the totalitarian descent by a more gradual route.

According to the concept of "utilitarian enframing," the individual is at the service of an oligarchy greedy for power and personal enrichment.

---

[8] "Enframing" refers here to German philosopher Martin Heidegger's notion of *Gestell.*—Trans.

[9] Yvan Blot, *L'oligarchie au pouvoir* (Paris: Éditions Economica, 2011).

In order to suitably fulfill his role as "raw material," the individual must be void of any roots: without race, without nation, and without religion. He must be void of an ideal; or rather his sole ideal must be simply the satisfaction of his needs. In morality, he must be relativistic so as to readily accept all tendencies of the ruling power and all attacks on human dignity when presented in a favorable light by the ruling power and justified by an inordinate appeal to emotions. Furthermore, the individual must be void of personality as of independent judgment. It is imperative that he conform to the movements of the crowd and not seek to be different. He must therefore "be brought up in a purely technical and utilitarian manner, without the general culture letting him think he is a free man."[10]

Such is the individual in a democracy. It is the composite of such individuals which is called the people. The intention, then, of democratic power is not to serve the good of the people, but to make use of the people for the good of the ruling oligarchy. From this vantage point, it is better for the individuals to no longer form a people at all, but rather a completely disposable and submissive human reserve. If this intention has not yet been fully realized, it is clear that it is well on its way to fulfillment. But it clashes with the reality of human nature, which rebels insofar as it is able in the face of its utilitarian debasement.

---

[10] Yvan Blot, "La façon dont l'oligarchie traite l'homme: une matière première," *Polémia*, October 4, 2009, http://archives.polemia.com/article.php?id=2393.

Chapter 2

THE RULING MINORITY

RULE by the people is completely impracticable. It is impossible for a people, like a single man, to issue an opinion, to cast a vote, to make a decision, etc. The people must have intermediaries and representatives, who will always be the true rulers in their place. Each voter, in a democracy, is the depositary of a tiny particle of sovereignty, in itself unusable. His sole power consists in dropping a ballot into a box, whereby he is immediately dispossessed of his particle of sovereignty at the profit of those who are going to represent him.

As long as democracy has existed, every means has been devised so that the "self-ruling" people have in practice almost nothing to say. A system established on false principles inevitably results in distortions which are at times quite far removed from these principles. In democracy, reality is contrary to what the principles proclaim: one can say that the majority almost never wins. Democracy is not the system of the majority, but that of the most powerful minority, and it has this power not simply due to its numbers, but also and above all due to its organization.

Democracy has produced a ruling class propped up by the political parties, whose foremost objective is the preservation of power. The elections, whose outcomes one seeks to restrict, are only a means for legitimizing the exercise of power. Once in place, the parties do not in the least seek to serve the common good, or rather they do so only if it first serves their own interest, which is to stay in and enjoy power.

The political parties are only a minority of the population. Whether they represent ideologies or social classes, or whatever segment of the population, whether they embody a fashion, a style, a type of discourse, or even just promises, they can never pretend to represent all of the population. Besides, their battle for power obliges them to pit people against each other, to seek out adherents, and to divide the population into rival factions. It would be naive to think that these parties, which derive their existence from division, would be capable (at least, insofar as they would like) of serving the common good. They can only claim to do so by imposing on the population their notion of the common good, which is the notion of their partisans, that is to say of a minority.

One might object that the political party members, those who appear on the ballots and thus those who are elected, owe their positions to their popularity and, consequently, that they must necessarily be representative of the largest possible segment of society. This view is perhaps applicable to very active parties which have not yet exercised power and have not yet been corrupted by it. In general, the political parties cease to function as representative organs at the moment they accede to power. They even work this transformation in their ranks by anticipation in order to be ready, according to their own criteria, to exercise power.

Personal popularity can help in a political party, but it can also exclude activists who risk overshadowing the strategists. Power exerts on many men and women a fascination which very few are capable of resisting, and these few do not generally get involved in democratic politics. The battle for power thus begins at the party level. It is there that the selection is made of who will be placed in an eligible position on the candidate list.[1] The criteria in this selection, however, are very far removed from what the voter typically imagines. One does not necessarily put forward someone who will faithfully adhere to the party's platform. Such a candidate is often idealistic. He might show himself to be firmly principled and uncompromising. He is unfit to rule in a democracy. The first quality of a candidate is not his ideals or his popularity, but his ability to betray ideals and to lie to the voters. This is useful to the party for it will enable it to maneuver itself so as to stay in power. It is this that will open the breach into which will rush the party backers, who are even less principled and certainly less popular. The goal of a political party is to conquer the state, to occupy it in the strategic sense of the word. It must be in control of the state's machinery and people its administration not simply to transform society, but above all to gain the maximum advantages for the party members.

---

[1] In proportional representation systems, where the number of party candidates who win seats is dependent on how well the party as a whole fares in the election, voters often have limited or sometimes no say about which party candidates will be given priority for a seat. Party leaders determine or influence the priority order. Candidates at the top of the party list who have a real chance of winning a seat are said to be in an "eligible" position.—Trans.

Much could be said about the psychology of political party candidates. The first thing one might notice is the metamorphosis of those who become political party members. If they have attended the meetings and registered as candidates, they have already crossed over mentally to the other side, to the side of power. They begin to reason like politicians, they start to justify abuses every citizen ought to be quick to condemn, and they become less sensitive to the foremost concerns of the people (even if they pretend the exact opposite). Their discourse becomes slippery. It is more and more out of step with that of the non-politicized people among whom they move about. The foremost concerns of their fellow citizens become less of a priority. They identify differently the evils from which society suffers and attribute to them causes other than those generally recognized. They go so far as to pretend that certain problems do not exist (such as high crime rates) or attribute erroneous causes to them (such as economic causes to high crime rates). Power, even before they exercise it, exerts on them a moral corruption and a mental deviancy. As soon as it does so, they no longer belong to the people who elected them, but to this machine of conquest for power that is the party.

The political parties put forward those of their members who show themselves to be the best manipulators. But among these, only those who are the most open to being manipulated themselves accede to power. It is therefore prudent to put aside, starting at the lowest echelons of the party, the idealistic activists who believe in the truth of the party platform and are prepared to dedicate their lives to putting it into practice. Such individuals risk compromising everything! They are useful to the base for inspiring confidence in the voters, but they must not attain power.

The ideal politician, on the other hand, is pliable, convincing, and a liar by instinct. He is not attached to any platform and has no ideological objective. The single thing to which he is truly committed is power. He wants its prestige and advantages, and seeks above all to be personally enriched by it. Any politician who presents this aspect is recognized as fit for power in a democracy. He will be esteemed by his peers, and they will extol his moderation, his knowledge of the issues, and his political savvy, which is only a way of camouflaging his passiveness and venality. It is therefore not surprising that democratically elected assemblies are almost exclusively comprised of these kinds of men and women. Elected heads of state almost always fit this profile, and international institutions, such as the European Union, consider it the only acceptable profile. Those not fitting this profile are "extremists."

Hence, Jean-Yves Le Gallou's take on the French presidential election of 2012:

> The voter is not there to choose the President of the Republic. His role is simply to lend a democratic legitimacy to a candidate deemed acceptable by the globalist superclass for representing its interests in France. There were real choices in the first round. There were no longer any in the second. Nicolas Sarkozy and François Hollande agree on the essentials: on the European bureaucratic regulations emanating from Brussels, on the subjection of French laws to judges of the European courts in Strasbourg and Luxembourg, on

military integration into NATO, on acceptance of the global free trade rules desired by the World Trade Organization, and on surrendering monetary sovereignty to the European Central Bank. Concerning all of this, Hollande or Sarkozy—where is there any room for maneuver? Aside from the heated rhetoric of one and the bodily demeanor of the other, what is the difference?[2]

The members of political parties form a political class. They are an organized minority who respond to their own motivations and who serve interests distinct from the common interest, interests arising from their proximity to power or their exercise thereof. Access to public funds is among their principal objectives. This political class acts all the more freely since there does not exist an arbiter in a democracy, or to be more exact, the one who ought to play the role of arbiter, the head of state, is himself a member of a party, generally the party in power. If he is not elected, as is the case for the king in a constitutional monarchy, he is deprived of any power and his role as arbiter is without effect.

This political class will tend towards autonomy vis-à-vis the electorate. In order to secure their dominant position, they will seek as much as possible to reduce electoral risk. They will do this through the use of the media and through regulatory mechanisms (such as allocating public funds only to parties having parliamentary seats, requiring a minimum 5% vote nationally to gain party representation in the legislature, imposing excessive ballot access rules on aspiring parties, etc.). But this hijacking of democracy

---

[2] Jean-Yves Le Gallou, "Le 6 mai je prendrai de l'altitude !," *Polémia*, April 25, 2012, http://archives.polemia.com/article.php?id=4778.

nevertheless requires some prudence on the part of the oligarchy. It is imperative to maintain the democratic rituals that give the elected, and therefore those who gain power, a kind of legitimacy. It is necessary to keep having the elections, the televised and parliamentary debates, as well as a certain form of opposition. However, these are only rituals. They are there in order to give the illusion of participation in power, not participation itself.

That democracy is the government of the minority rather than the majority is also easily observed through the statistical analysis of elections. The first factor necessary to take into account is the abstention rate, which can be as high as 30% of the electorate. This means that the percentage of votes obtained by a candidate or a party is not based on 100, but on 70. Now, the voters do not themselves comprise the entire population, for it is necessary to subtract those who are not allowed to vote, principally under-age minors, who are considered electorally non-existent. This portion represents about 15% of the population. This means the percentage of votes obtained in an election is in reality based on only 55% of the total population if one subtracts 30% for abstainers and 15% for under-age minors.

During an election, the winning parties generally win 20% to 30% of the votes cast. Let us say it is 30%. Of a base of 55%, which is the actual rate of the population that participates, the party amasses only 16.5% of the total population's votes. If one is opposed to family suffrage and only wants to account for the abstention rate, this score goes up to 21% of the total population.

In the European elections of 2009, 56.59% of the European population did not vote. That was an increase of 2% when compared to 2004. This abstention rate would have been even slightly higher if voting were not compulsory in Belgium and Luxembourg. It rose to 59% in France. Such a level of abstention obviously calls into question the representativeness of the European parliament. Its sitting members in effect represent less than half of all Europeans.

In the United States presidential election of 2008, the Democratic candidate obtained 53% of the vote compared to 46% for the Republican candidate, with 80 million Americans (26.6% of the population) not voting. In 2012, the Democratic candidate obtained 51% of the vote compared to 47% for the Republican candidate, with a lower participation rate than in 2008.

In France, the abstention rate is still more telling. In the presidential elections of 2002, Jacques Chirac obtained 19.8% of the vote and Jean-Marie Le Pen 16.8% in the first round. With the rate of abstention being 28.4%, the real percentage obtained by candidate Chirac was therefore down at 14.26%. That means only this small portion of the French population actually wanted Jacques Chirac as president. The fact that he obtained 82.21% in the second round is, of course, misleading, as he only owed this remarkable showing to the candidate he was up against and the media hype with which the French electorate was bombarded. Therefore, a mere 15% of the French people wanted Jacques Chirac in the Élysée Palace.

In the presidential elections of 2007, Nicolas Sarkozy obtained 31.18% of the vote in the first round and 53.06% in the second round. The rate of abstention in both rounds was close to 16%, which brings the percentages down to 26.19 for the first round and 44.57 for the second. Less than one in two French persons wanted Nicolas Sarkozy in the Élysée Palace. In 2012, 20% of the French did not vote in the first round. The two competing candidates each garnered no more than 30% of the votes cast. In reality, each of them received only 24% of the vote from the electorate.

More recently, in the second round of the 2017 French presidential elections, the abstention rate rose to 26%, with about an additional 8% of eligible voters casting blank or invalid protest ballots. As a result, Emmanuel Macron won the presidency not with 66% of the vote, but with 44% only, less than half of the French electorate.

Parliamentary systems do not impose minimum participation quotas beneath which the results would be deemed invalid. Such a practice would considerably weaken the system. Thus, elections where the abstention rate would rise to 50%, 60%, or even 80% would remain valid. Those who abstain are considered to be indifferent and, consequently, accepting of any result whatsoever.

It is, of course, a convenient way to dismiss the problem, for no one knows why the electorate is not voting. Those in power do not seem too concerned by the phenomenon of abstentionism, for they conduct no investigations to determine the reasons that cause voters to abstain from voting. Whatever the reasons, a democracy where 20% of the population refuses to vote is a democracy that is ill. In China and Vietnam, people are put into prison because they demand the right to vote. In Europe, a portion of the population seems to have learned the true nature of the system and asserts that "voting is really of no use."

Abstentionism lifts a corner of the veil. It is an important indicator. Far from being indifferent to election results, abstentionists consider it useless to vote, either because the candidate of their choice has no chance of winning or because, in their eyes, the country will be governed in the same way regardless of the winning candidate. If this intuition were verified, it would demonstrate that abstentionists implicitly recognize the oligarchic nature of the democratic system. They perceive that beyond partisan rivalries there exists among the parties an agreement on the essentials: the state's centralized power, the defense of democratic principles, and the "availability" of elected officials to their real bosses.

Regardless, the numbers from recent elections show that those elected never represent the majority of the population. It is necessary, in order to have an absolute majority, to have exceptional historical circumstances. But when a party obtains an absolute majority, it can be tempted to put an end to the democratic system. Democracy is never protected from self-destruction. When the parties are too weak, it is the rule of the minority; when they are too powerful, they compromise the system. In both cases, democracy shows itself to be impossible.

During almost all of the nineteenth century, European countries practiced censitary suffrage, which gave the right to vote to the wealthy only. A minority electorate voted and was represented. The institution of universal suffrage only displaced the problem. Parliaments have splintered themselves into more numerous parties so that obtaining the absolute majority has become unrealistic. It is the return, in another form, to the principle of the minority, from which democracy seems unable to escape.

Coalition governments, at first glance, represent a solution to this problem. The parties that are more significant but unable to obtain more than fifty percent of the vote form an alliance in order to together constitute a majority in the parliament. These coalitions can bring together two, three, or even more parties.

The British, who had been used to having only one party in power at a time, seemed at a loss from 2010 to 2015 when the Conservatives had to ally themselves with the Liberal Democrats in a coalition government. Governing seemed to them difficult, even impossible, in those conditions. That is, however, how the Netherlands, Belgium, and Austria normally govern themselves, or at least how they try. The coalition system claims to be more democratic because it relies on a larger base in the parliament and thus claims to represent a more significant portion of the population. This portion is rarely a majority. When a coalition brings together a majority in the parliament, it is likely that, in light of the abstention rate, this majority does not represent the true majority of the population. But this is not where the problem lies. A coalition government is obliged to water down its wine. Each party entering into a government accord gives up a portion of its political platform. The parliamentary majority is obtained in exchange for marginalizing programs of each party, which comes back to saying that the principle of the minority again triumphs. Let us say that three parties form a coalition government, and that each of them, to make the coalition viable, gives up a third of its electoral platform, which is tantamount to no longer representing the voters for whom this third was important. This coalition, even if it achieves a majority in the parliament, no longer represents the totality of the electorate that voted for the parties that constitute it.

It is therefore impossible for a coalition government to claim it represents the majority of the population. Each time a party in such a government gives up this or that item of its platform, it betrays a portion of its voters. In a country like Belgium where the coalition system is practiced, the parties are in communication with each other *before* the elections and are making agreements without the voters' knowledge. The electoral race therefore becomes a joke, as the games seem to be played ahead of time. If the voters were aware of the alliances weaved in the shadows, it is likely they would change their votes. That is why these meetings are held in secret. By acting in this way, the parties recognize they are betraying the voters before as well as after the elections. The purpose of the election is not to know the public's opinion, but to give the parties legitimacy, something which is looked on with growing skepticism, however.

In every case, one sees that democracy gravitates towards a minority, oligarchic system. It is essential to understand that this tendency is not a happenstance of democracy which can be corrected or avoided through some structural modifications. This is a very popular misconception to believe that democracy can know abuses in spite of principles universally recognized as true. This error is kept alive in the public's mind to meet the needs of the cause. People's sense of dissatisfaction is growing, but that they lose hope in democracy and turn away from it must especially not be allowed to happen. It is thus vital for those who exercise power in a democracy to admit that democracy is not in the best of health, since this is strikingly evident wherever one looks, but to also clarify that this is only accidental and that democratic principles remain the best that man has discovered for self-governance.

This reasoning seduces many people who sincerely condemn the oligarchic orientation of the present-day Establishment, without requiring them to admit that democracy itself is a bad political system. But this is only a deception contrived by those who want to keep themselves in power: "Believe in us! We are going to straighten things out for you!"

Democracy, then, is not ill by accident. It is so in principle. The principles of democracy are false and impracticable. Their application can only produce grave aberrations and human disasters.

One might still believe that democracy has only been found aberrant in its practice. But this also is a convenient falsehood. The reality is that democracy was invented *for the purpose of* bringing an oligarchy into power and keeping it there. The history of the establishment of the parliamentary monarchy in Great Britain, as well as the histories of the French and Russian revolutions, confirm the determination of a social class or a group of people representing an ideology or particular interests to seize power for their advantage by forcing it, insofar as possible, from the hands of the impartial arbiter—from the monarch. Wherever this phenomenon occurs, under the pretext of serving the good of the people and bringing them liberty, there are powerful minorities, often rich, who seize the levers of power in order to make them work for their own interests.

But what distinguishes parliamentary democracies is that these interest groups do not act directly. In a communist or fascist regime, one at least knows who is in power, what the prevailing ideology is, and what interests are favored. These latter regimes, despite their brutality, do not hide their game. It is not the same for parliamentary democracy, in which the driving forces are not those seen on the political stage, and in which the ultimate beneficiaries do not step out into the media spotlight.

In their competition for power, the political parties are supported by money powers. These are, in a democracy, always more powerful than the political power, for they exist before, during, and after the period when the parties exercise their rule. If one wonders why economics trump politics in a democracy, the answer is easily found in the permanence of financial powers in relation to the ephemeral character of political power. The latter is always broken up into limited terms of office, always needing to be won again, never acquired for a long time. This is one of the principal weaknesses of democracy. Faced with this, the political power finds economic, financial, and commercial actors, whose power is not dependent upon elections or terms of office, and which continues indefinitely, free of major setbacks and even independent of individual persons. Economics enjoys a definite advantage here. The political parties are always in need of money for their campaigns, and they are not self-supporting. They inevitably resort to depending on those who can support them financially. What is more, the democratic politician is par excellence someone who sells himself. He is not impartial; he is torn by a double game of popularity and his power is always of short duration. He is therefore tempted to draw the maximum profit from his brief time in power.

The democratic ruler is not the owner of his power; he is only its temporary holder. He therefore does not have the natural inclination to maintain the value of the assets of the country he governs as would a hereditary monarch. The latter behaves as an owner interested in the good state of public and private affairs since, not having merely been lent a short-term motive of self-interest, he and his descendants are to benefit in the long-term. The prosperity and freedom the nation enjoys, as well as its degree of contentment, are not inconsequential to the monarch, who glories in and benefits from them. The democratic ruler does not have this concern. He behaves like a renter who enjoys a good for a short period of time and is unconcerned about its long-term value.[3] This attitude is made easy by the democratic individualism that is pervasive among the population. The individual in a democracy

---

[3] See Hans-Hermann Hoppe, *Democracy: The God that Failed* (New Brunswick, NJ: Transaction Publishers, 2007), 45-50.

"acts in total anonymity, secrecy and legal irresponsibility,"[4] as do his rulers.

After all, the democratic ruler is protected by his unaccountability. He need not ever render an account of his lawfully made decisions once his term has ended. He is protected by the parliamentary majority, which dispenses him from truly considering the best way to pursue the common good. For this reason, he is prone to take lightly decisions whose effects will not be felt until after the end of his term. National debt is the most typical example of this democratic unaccountability, which involves future generations.

The democratic politician, because of his short-term interest and his unaccountability, is therefore corruptible by vocation. Nothing predisposes him to govern in a disinterested fashion; on the contrary, he is driven to draw the maximum profit from his position of power. One will therefore be on guard, at the party level, to not let accede to posts of political consequence any man or woman whose moral rigidity or ideology would pose an obstacle to party backers.

The money powers—by this term is meant the large industrial and commercial groups, the energy and armament markets, and the banks—who do not form the majority of the population and operate as hidden minorities, seek to use political power, by means of proxies, to serve their own interests. It is the money powers that are the true masters of the democratic state. It is they, ultimately, who make the

---

[4] Erik von Kuehnelt-Leddihn, *Liberty or Equality* (Front Royal, VA: Christendom Press, 1993), 150.

long-term decisions, present their viewpoints, and dictate the major courses of action of governments.

Some people believe political power *sometimes* compromises with the money powers, but ultimately maintains its independence. That is an error. It is the money powers that have the last word and the compromising of political parties is constant. The reason for this is first of all structural. Political power is weak because its terms of office are short, ever to be renewed and always uncertain. It is only exercised inside national borders. The political class, even if it is certain to attain power, does not know, however, in what proportions this power will be distributed among its constituent parties. No politician can be sure his term will be renewed. Furthermore, politicians are very sensitive about their image, and a false step, a revelation made about their corruption or fraud, can be fatal for them. In contrast with this weakness, the money powers enjoy continuity in time and the great advantage of not being bound by political borders. That is why the large international groups are so powerful. If they encounter an obstacle in one country, they turn to another. They negotiate their presence or departure, which means work or unemployment for the population. The money powers very often own the media, through which they are able to play a decisive role in public opinion, on which politicians depend. As their business turnover is sometimes greater than the GDP of democratic states, they have no difficulty putting the latter in a vulnerable position.

The money powers have the money, in other words the most powerful and universal means in this world of manipulating people. They can corrupt politicians and finance electoral campaigns. It is they who hold the levers of democracy.

Political power, in a democracy, always thus has a tendency to grow weak and the money powers to grow stronger. The latter, however, will keep watch so that this is not seen, lest there be a popular movement rendering political power inaccessible to their advances, thereby harming their interests. It is in the vital interest of the two partners, the corrupter and the corrupted, to keep their agreements secret. What is more evident today is the extent of the media's submission to the political power and the money powers. That is why the general public knows practically nothing of these dealings and, when they do accidentally come to light, the political power is able to easily denounce them as baseless calumnies.

Information does still leak out, however. With the world of the media more and more paralyzed by the tyranny of political correctness and, for this reason, presenting a completely biased view of the world, the internet has become the principal source of free information.

It is necessary to distinguish between two kinds of corruption in a democracy. The first kind is *external corruption*, which is that exercised by the money powers (multinational organizations, banks, interest groups, and lobbies) on the political power. This form of corruption is supposed to remain secret when it evolves into illegality, and discreet when it remains within the limits of acceptability. To receive an envelope in order to amend the contents of a future law is illegal. On the other hand, to be offered a vacation on the Turkish Riviera is not necessarily so.

The preliminary phase of external corruption occurs by means of lobbying groups. These groups are extremely numerous and particularly abound in the places where the laws are voted on. Their mission is to influence lawmakers through appropriate but biased information which will swing decisions in the direction of their interests. They keep watch so as to position themselves favorably from the moment parliamentary committees are formed, realizing that the initial account presented of an issue, even if it is subsequently reshaped, can still maintain afterwards a certain authority in the minds of the lawmakers. It is necessary to keep in mind here that the lawmakers are not experts on the issues they are discussing. Generally, they are even completely ignorant of the matters with which they are dealing. They are male and female politicians, without any particular training and whose level of instruction is at times mediocre. These people need to form an opinion, be able to participate on a committee, and possibly respond to journalists. The lobbying groups prepare them for this by providing basic information which anticipates and gives some figures for the most common objections.

The less transparent democracy is, the more active lobbying is. Throughout the lawmaking process, the lobbyists are at work in a real race for influence. One would be mistaken to underestimate their role in the drafting and passage of a law. In the European Union, lobbying is an inescapable practice. Those without recourse to it have already lost and, of course, only the richest and best organized groups come out on top. According to the most recent estimates, there are some 15,000 to 30,000 lobbyists for various associations, companies, special interests, and ideological groups swarming like flies around the European Parliament.[5] Several thousand lobby offices are set up permanently in Brussels. A large portion of them are accredited at the European Parliament and even subsidized by the European Union, which says much about their influence.

Such a concentration proves that lobbying yields results and reveals the true interests championed by lawmakers. The delegates seated in Brussels and Strasbourg are far from their voters and under sufficiently little media spotlight. It is the lobbies that determine their votes in the assemblies. Among the represented interests, 75% are of an industrial nature. This explains, for example, the European Union's favorable position towards GMOs when the vast majority of Europeans are opposed to them.

When lobbying parliamentarians is not enough or the decision has passed to the executive authority, the pressure groups and money powers have recourse to active corruption. This can be a lunch at a restaurant, a vacation of astronomical cost, a cruise on a luxury yacht, a "helping hand" in a delicate situation, or even more simply, an envelope. The entire political class operates this way. These practices are standard.

It is corruption that so well explains the absurd, unjustifiable, and downright scandalous decisions made by the European political deciders, such as the mass purchase of vaccines for a completely phony

---

[5] Corporate Europe Observatory, *Lobby Planet Brussels—The EU Quarter*, 4th ed. (Brussels: Corporate Europe Observatory, 2011), http://corporateeurope.org/sites/default/files/publications/ceolobbylow.pdf.

epidemic,[6] or even Turkey's candidacy for European Union membership when it was overwhelmingly rejected by the population.

The second form of corruption is what one would call *internal corruption*, or even *self-corruption*. It is the state that corrupts its own political personnel by obtaining from them a greater docility and getting them to close their eyes to anything that would shock a normally formed conscience. For such a practice, democratic institutions are particularly fitting, as there is no arbiter in a democracy. If the role of arbiter were to be played by the parliament, one would corrupt the parliamentarians, which appears to be an extremely easy thing to do. No assembly has ever refused to vote itself a pay increase.

The pay and multiple benefits of democratic political personnel are in general very poorly known, and the numbers are not easy to obtain. The government tends to hide them for the reason that they are, rightly so, very unpopular. However, the pay and benefits, as they do not correspond proportionally to any professional obligations, are the best guarantee of the system's stability. Not only the complicity of the political personnel and the civil servants is effortlessly obtained, but there is also a sense created of belonging to a caste, a privileged elite cut off from the rest of the world by the fact that they enjoy a standard of living

---

[6] In 2009, the French Minister of Health, Roselyne Bachelot, ordered 94 million doses of the H1N1 influenza vaccine. Soon afterwards, the World Health Organization announced that the declared pandemic was already over. No outbreak had yet occurred in France, and only 5.6 million French had been vaccinated. Most of the vaccine doses were destroyed. The cost to French taxpayers for the purchase and disposal of the vaccine amounted to 400 million euros.

that is disproportionate to the rest of society. Nothing is more effective than money for producing this sense, and nothing corrupts a conscience more quickly than money. As a human being cannot live long-term with a sense of guilt, the system's favored ones think up all kinds of justifications for their hefty salaries and the multiple benefits which go along with them. For this same reason, they seek out the company of one another, or of very well-off people, so as not to have constantly before their eyes the injustice from which they benefit.

Nothing cuts political personnel off more from social and political reality than enjoying the benefits of the system, and it is indispensable to the moral and intellectual "availability" of these personnel that they be cut off from the reality in which the rest of the population lives.

The class sentiment that develops in a democracy, due to its internal corruption, contributes to the strengthening of the reigning oligarchy, which is democracy's natural orientation. This oligarchy could never last if it were confronted with a standing indictment from a truly free and representative parliament. It has sufficed, therefore, even if it does result from a long process, to subjugate political personnel and civil servants by purchasing their consciences. The selections made within political parties facilitate having particularly well-disposed political personnel.

It follows that the state, in its national form or even in the form of a supranational organization, is nothing more than machinery in the operation of the world's major financial, industrial, and commercial interests.

It is no longer in the parliamentary assemblies or in the governments that the major decisions affecting the fate of peoples or the future of societies are made. These decisions are made at the head of major money powers which hold consultative meetings that are sometimes public (such as the G7, G8, and G20) and sometimes secret (such as the Bilderberg Group), and which make use of proxy organizations such as the United Nations, the International Monetary Fund, the World Health Organization, the World Trade Organization, the World Bank, the Council of Europe, the European Union, etc.

The opinion of voters has no weight and must not interfere. It is necessary only to take care to favorably prepare public opinion through the conduit of the media, in order that it accept as good or normal something it would instinctively reject if it were not conditioned.

Democracy is the political system that enables organized minorities to hold power the most firmly and the most durably, even more so if they are rich. Universal suffrage, therefore, does not constitute progress when compared to censitary suffrage, for the representatives are further removed from the people. Under the system of censitary suffrage, the power to make laws is concentrated in the hands of the country's financial elite. But the interests of this elite are still partially tied to the common good. Hence, there is a kind of stability in this system. In a system of universal suffrage, of course, anyone can vote and sit in the parliament, but the money powers will apply themselves to corrupting the elected and turning their activity away from serving the common good, if that had ever been their intention. Thus, owing to its lack of an independent and impartial arbiter, it would appear parliamentary democracy is marked by an inevitable orientation towards plutocracy, from which it has no means of escape.

Chapter 3

TOTALITARIAN DEMOCRACY

THE description of the democratic system, if one has been following it thus far, provokes a sense of disgust that is quite natural. Too many injustices are committed in the name of democracy, too many abuses of power, and especially too many particular interests are served by the state and international institutions and organizations, whose vocation ought to be serving the common good and the interest of all without distinction. Democracy is not the system which suits such a noble objective. If it has been presented as such in the past, back when one might have sincerely believed that accidental deviations were insufficient to condemn an entire system, one can no longer today consider democracy a system fit to serve the common interest.

Public sentiment is averse, however, to arriving at such a conclusion. It has been conditioned so much against any other form of government and it has become so convinced that democracy, in spite of its weaknesses, is the system of humanity par excellence, that it cannot admit that this sure system could also be, like so many others, called into question.

If it is to be admitted that democracy is full of defects, and even that it is unable to be reformed, let us at least maintain it despite everything, for it is the best guarantee against a totalitarian state! This argument is very often presented as the one which must save democracy before its detractors. Democracy would be the best safeguard against any totalitarian regime and, for this reason alone, it would deserve to be maintained and protected. This view is false. It is a trap, moreover, which ensnares public opinion, blinded as it is by the media, a statist education system, and a general conditioning that is pervasive in contemporary Western culture.

First of all, it is dishonest to present the modern-day citizen with this choice between only two political systems: democracy or totalitarian government. These two forms of government are recent systems. Democracy itself, as we know it, is only a bit more than two centuries old, irrespective of the form of suffrage in place. In most European countries, universal suffrage does not date back beyond a century. Humanity, then, has been governed under other systems for periods of time much longer than this democratic interlude. To put this one and only alternative before people amounts to invalidating centuries, and even millennia, of political experience. The presentation is not only dishonest, but it is precisely also of a totalitarian nature, for it does not allow the intellect the ability to freely inform itself through the evaluation of undistorted information.

The second reason why this choice between either democracy or totalitarianism is to be rejected is that democracy is itself also totalitarian. To turn away from communism and fascism in order to throw oneself into the arms of democracy is to flee the bear and the wolf for the boa constrictor. It is to fail to recognize the totalitarian foundations of democracy because one prefers to believe in its promises of liberty and to subscribe to the calumnies it heaps on its rivals.

It is necessary to recall here that the totalitarian governments which were established in the twentieth century all had their origins in democracy. All were born of electoral systems, and some of them conquered the state with the most perfect democratic legality. Dictatorial regimes, such as those of Napoleon, Hitler, and Lenin, were born in parliamentary lands where democracy reveled. Democracy was of no harm to them, it did not forestall them; on the contrary, it served them. These historical examples can be abundantly detailed and illustrated. One must not forget that the only dictatorial government known under the Ancien Régime was the one under Cromwell, champion of the parliamentary cause and author of the first genocide in modern history. Parliamentary democracy has been the ideal pathway to totalitarian and dictatorial regimes.

What could be more natural given that parliamentary democracy and its totalitarian cousins trace their roots back to the French Revolution, that great rupture in civilization and the first modern age totalitarian experience.

The very foundations of democracy are of a totalitarian nature. Democracy is the system in which anything is legitimate from the moment it is wanted by the majority. Democracy, knowing neither good nor evil but only numbers, does not recoil from any decision or law that would be voted on democratically. In a tyranny, the tyrant abuses his power and knows it. He cannot claim as legitimate those decisions which strike the populace, because he alone makes them and has to confront the people's disavowal, even if it goes unspoken. The tyrant can never be morally justified to act in the name of everyone or in the interest of all, for he has no mandate and does not respect the natural law. His power rests on force alone, not on justice or general consent. In democracy, however, the guarantee of general consent—in reality the consent of the majority or the most powerful minority—supports the decisions of the political power and justifies them to such an extent that the democratic government considers itself exempt from assuming the consequences of its acts. It has the backing of the majority, who gives it cover and whose will it is simply carrying out. Thus, the Nazis, losing the war and seeing the human disasters the defeat had brought about, pointed the voters back to their choice: if they did not want what they got, they should have voted differently.

The politician in a democracy, whether he is a parliamentarian or a minister, is totally unaccountable. Responsibility for his decisions is assumed by those who elected him. His accountability is atomized among the millions of voters who have only themselves to blame if they are dissatisfied. The minister of a government is accountable to the parliament, and the parliamentarians to the voters. Each one can exonerate himself on the basis of those who give him backing. It is an organized escape from accountability. Hence, there is the customary casualness of elected politicians with respect to the duties of their office and to the benefits it procures them. These are people who do not acknowledge their mistakes in the exercise of their duties, let alone resign when they are pointed out, for they look to benefit from a blank check from their voters.

Modern democratic systems do not have, like the democracy of ancient Athens, a kind of tribunal which assesses the quality and consequences of decisions made by the magistrates. Some of them, at the end of their term, had to pay out of pocket for the harm caused by their bad decisions. There is no such thing in modern democracy, where the minister risks nothing more than losing his post, not even his pension.

As if this were not enough, the scope of law in a democracy must theoretically be unlimited. Under the Ancien Régime, the law was not at the monarch's disposal, for most rules of common life were fixed by custom, over which the monarch had hardly any power. But in a democracy, not only is the law considered to apply to everyone indifferently—which is not truly the case, since a multitude of new privileges exist which have restored de facto inequality before the law—but it also applies in all matters. Democratic parliaments can make and undo laws as they please, and their scope of action is unlimited, which is logical since nothing must be an obstacle to the will of the self-ruling people. It is not strange, therefore, to see the state regulate domains which are within the realm of tradition and antecedent to it, like the transmission of surnames or rules of orthography. It should not be surprising that the modern democratic state decrees that the human fetus is not a human being or that certain opinions judged to be incorrect send the one expressing them to prison. More recently, one has seen the democratic state, in order to remedy the financial crisis it itself provoked, raise the retirement age by several years—so easily does it dispose some of the living years of its citizens. The democratic state can euthanize the elderly and the demented, it can legalize drugs, and it can enable homosexual couples to adopt children. It can infringe on private property and tax without limit. The natural law does not constitute an obstacle for it. It can regulate everything, change everything, and even envisage reshaping man himself, through education, the media, the law, and advertising. Its power is limitless as long as society does not fall into revolution or chaos. It does not need to justify itself to do this. It does not need a police force. It suffices for it to rely on the support of a parliamentary majority.

The current notion of a "legal vacuum" is symptomatic of this legal totalitarianism, since it presupposes that no means exist for handling a problem of social life outside the framework of the voted law. The citizen is thus considered as lacking any judgment or good sense, and therefore incapable of discovering what is just outside of the law. The "legal vacuum" is very convenient, of course, for it justifies state intervention in everything. The democratic state, therefore, is far from following the counsel of Montesquieu, according to whom a small number of laws is the guarantee of greater individual freedom. Wherever the "legal vacuum" exists, the domain of personal responsibility and good sense begins. But the democratic state has no use for responsible citizens capable of exercising their judgment. It prefers to extend its empire over docile and dependent citizens. It prefers that the people seek to know what is permitted and forbidden rather than what is good and bad. The first attitude requires submission, while the second requires freedom.

Can the 1948 Universal Declaration of Human Rights protect the citizen in a democracy from an abuse of state power? Absolutely not. Human rights are appealed to in a purely opportunistic fashion: when something is troublesome, they are invoked; in other cases, one keeps quiet about them. Furthermore, the Universal Declaration of Human Rights is a very imperfect document, and its imperfection was likely intended. It maintains a certain confusion between human rights (such as the right to life, the freedom of movement, the freedom of expression, and the right to property) and the rights a person might enjoy as the citizen of a state (such as the rights to social security, leisure, and paid leave). It makes no distinction between rights and needs, so housing, for example, which is a human need, is presented as a right. No mention is made of individual responsibility.

But what makes this declaration a flagrant example of democratic hypocrisy is that it assigns to the democratic state the role of arbiter for human rights (Article 29). If a citizen of a democratic state, then, is the victim of a human rights violation, he cannot hope to have the government of his own country condemned, for the laws oppressing him were voted democratically. Everything passes as if a democratically voted law could never, by definition, violate human rights. It very often happens that democratic governments do infringe on human rights (the right to property, the right to life, the freedom of opinion and expression), but in no case will a court consider this infringement as such, for the law responsible for the charged violation was voted democratically. "Human rights" show themselves, therefore, to be an ally of the state against the individual rather than the other way around.

Democratic governments have shown time and again with what contempt they regard human rights. They show themselves very accommodating on the matter when it comes to countries having oil (such as Saudi Arabia and Sudan) or countries offering a market for commerce and industry (such as China), but all of a sudden demand human rights when it is a matter of bringing down a rival. They are clearly biased.

It is also interesting to note how often human rights are invoked for hegemonic or imperialistic ends. Human rights are a purely Western invention inspired by Enlightenment philosophy; they advocate individualism and secularism and have a materialistic view of the human being. But Western governments have no scruples practicing a form of neocolonialism in imposing human rights on countries or peoples totally foreign to Western culture and for whom the human rights ideology represents alienation more than liberation.

One cannot therefore count on human rights to act in opposition to the totalitarian orientations of democracy, for it is they that give democracy a philosophical basis which is presented as universal truth.

Democracy tends towards totalitarian government through legal pretensions designed as substitutions for morality. A government which does not recognize any moral law and for which good and evil do not exist, but only the will of numbers, opens before itself a field free to manipulation and oppression. In democracy, good and evil must become one with the law, for it is inadmissible that there should exist something superior to the law. From the moment there would exist moral principles over which the law has no power, that would amount to saying democracy accepts something as "more sovereign" than the will of the majority. Nothing though can trump the sovereignty of the people. It follows that the law, which is the expression of the will of the majority—at least in theory—has to encompass the entire moral domain and cannot tolerate a moral reference which would be external to it. It is for this reason that democracy inevitably evolves towards legal totalitarianism.

And, in fact, democratic citizens are behaving more and more like beings submitted to a law rather than beings endowed with reason and a critical intellect who are capable of determining for themselves what is just and unjust. They seek rather to know what is allowed and forbidden. It is striking to see how quickly a democratic population accepts as normal acts which it considered immoral, simply because they have become legal. Thus, wearing a safety belt inside a car has become a moral act because it is a legal obligation. Not insuring oneself when insurance is obligatory borders on immorality. Abortion and euthanasia, which revolted our grandparents, have become morally acceptable since being decriminalized. The salaries paid to political personnel, which constitutes an odious scandal in states claiming to be egalitarian, are generally accepted and at times even justified because they are legal.

In democracy, the law has the tendency to take the place of morality, and the people have the tendency to look solely to the law for determining what is good and evil, what is just and unjust. The concept of an "unjust law" is increasingly becoming a foreign notion in democracy.

Formerly, one considered recourse to numbers as a reliable guarantee against any overstep by the state. It was impossible, one thought, that the majority be mistaken or that the state deceive the majority. If such a situation happened, it could not last. But these ideas date from a time when the population still had a moral code, traditions, and a judgment very much their own, which the state had not yet fashioned. There existed from this fact many fewer laws and, consequently, many more occasions for exercising one's moral judgment. But today, things have very much changed. The state does not cease to fill "legal vacuums" and to legislate in a bulimic fashion, to such an extent that the laws become entangled and end up contradicting each other, so that more and more specialized lawyers are needed and, of course, the ordinary people are totally incapable of making sense of these laws.

In this, also, the democratic state renders the population more and more dependent upon it. It even gets them accustomed to a kind of arbitrariness and caprice, by subjecting them to a complex legal apparatus that is omnipresent and in constant evolution.

This legal uncertainty, in which the population finds itself, can only favor criminality. There, where the law changes, all while claiming to reflect the good, traditional moral reference points disappear and crime proliferates. What is more, the democratic state, in seeking to make the law a norm of behavior without having itself become a model of justice, only aggravates citizens' distrust towards it; these citizens will tend to justify their disrespect for the law by pointing to the injustice and scandals of which the state is guilty.

The last totalitarian advance of the democratic state in legislative matters has probably passed too unnoticed. Perhaps it is necessary to see in this a fatalistic sign for populations with respect to the omnipotence of a state which tends towards reducing individual freedoms. The "anti-discrimination" laws, in fact, represent a considerable encroachment on individual liberties, even though they are justified in part by these liberties. Discriminating is a function natural to man. It is an act which follows from the use of reason. Every day we discriminate dozens of times by choosing according to our own personal criteria what suits us and rejecting what does not. To prevent or criminalize this natural process for the reason that it might be offensive to certain people is a dangerous reduction of liberty. The democratic state presents anti-discriminatory measures as a means for protecting minorities against abuse of the majority's dominant position. Few people have seen just how much this reason is hypocritical and a mere pretext for extending the state's power.

When an owner offers an apartment for rent, he has, in a free society, the right to determine himself, outside of any constraint, whom he wishes to accept as a tenant. From the moment he is the owner, he enjoys this right in the same way that he can decorate his apartment according to his taste, remodel it, sell it, live in it himself, or farm snails in it. If these different uses of his property are not causing the neighbors any nuisance, his liberty is total. He also thus has the liberty to refuse tenants who are not to his taste because they are vegetarian, German, Catholic, or homosexual, or for whatever other reason. He does not even have the obligation to justify his refusal.

In a democratic society, there is not this liberty. The owner is constrained by law—and note well that the discrimination is presented as highly immoral—to accept no matter what tenant from the moment he presents the guarantees of credit-worthiness required by law. This prohibition against discrimination is imposed in the name of equality, of human dignity, and so forth, so that it is difficult for the owner who wants to defend his rights not to feel a sense of guilt.

The trouble though caused by this discrimination is negligible. The vegetarian, the German, the Catholic, or the homosexual turned away by this owner will not have trouble finding an apartment rented out by an owner who has the same characteristic as he or who would be indifferent to this characteristic. In fact, there is no lack of vegetarian, German, Catholic, or homosexual owners in the real estate market. If these groups are minorities in society, the demand coming from tenant candidates belonging to one of these groups will inevitably meet with a proportional supply. One does not see then where the harm is. It is certainly very unpleasant to see the door shut in one's face because one is a vegetarian, a

German, or whatever, but this unpleasantness can be easily avoided, by allowing, let us say, the owner to advertise his tenant criteria.

On the other hand, the harm caused to individual liberty by anti-discrimination laws is immense. The right to property is diminished by the law and the value of the asset is lessened. Once the owner no longer has total authority over his own property, it is less advantageous for him to be the owner. The law forbids him certain uses of his own property and, from this fact, this property becomes less appealing. The owner who discriminates between tenant candidates is, at first glance, hurting himself, for he is reducing the demand. But, from his point of view, it is the opposite that occurs, for it seems to him his property would lose some of its value were he to accept a vegetarian or a German, etc. It matters little that this point of view might be absurd, for a thing's value is a subjective notion.

But what is especially dangerous—all the more dangerous because it has passed unnoticed—is that the right to discriminate, which is removed from the private individual, is assumed by the state. While the state forbids discrimination, it is itself discriminating. The right of the owner is transferred to the state, which can thenceforth declare what forms of discrimination are acceptable (for example, discrimination against smokers, historical revisionists, or members of extremist parties, since the state is in an apparent fight against tobacco use, historical revisionism,[1] and

---

[1] In many European democracies, publicly denying or downplaying the official account of certain historical events, most notably the Holocaust, is illegal and punishable by fine or prison.—Trans.

extremism) and what forms of discrimination are unacceptable. But this is still only of minor harm. More serious still is the discrimination exercised by the state itself. By taking away the right of owners to discriminate, the state is doing nothing other than discriminating against them at the profit of the tenants. Thus, the state creates two categories of persons, owners and tenants, who are not entitled to the same rights. The first cannot discriminate between tenant candidates while the second can discriminate between owner candidates. In the contract which is to bring them together, the owners are disadvantaged by the state.

The same goes for businesses which find themselves forbidden to discriminate in hiring. No one knows better the best profile for a position than the business which is offering the position. So the business is allowed to discriminate on the basis of qualifications or age, but it is forbidden to do so on the basis of sex, skin color, or religion. The state considers these criteria to be inappropriate. But why should it be the state who decides this? By depriving the business of this fundamental freedom to choose with whom it wants to work, the state causes it considerable harm. It brings about a loss of wealth since the business is thenceforth obliged to work with employees it would not have chosen had it been able to act freely.

The state that forbids discrimination according to sex and wants to impose parity on every level infringes gravely on the freedom of individuals and businesses, in complete violation of the principle of subsidiarity. It must be noted that the state's criteria is of an arbitrary nature, thus a matter of political ideology rather than of simple justice. The state forbids salary discrimination according to sex, but it allows and practices discrimination according to age, since it remunerates its civil servants differently according to their seniority. Why would age be a more valid criterion than sex?

The discrimination practiced by private individuals is of little consequence and the harm caused is negligible. But the discrimination practiced by the state is clearly of an entirely different nature, for it has a general impact on all of society. When the state discriminates, everyone is affected and the discrimination is incorporated into law. If there is indeed then a discrimination which is unacceptable because it produces devastating consequences on account of its scope and its legal force, it is precisely that practiced by the state. Now, if one takes a closer look at this, the state is discriminating unceasingly. It discriminates against owners to the benefit of tenants; it discriminates against businesses to the benefit of employees; it discriminates between employees and the self-employed; it discriminates between civil servants and the rest of the population; it discriminates between public services and private businesses. It discriminates against consumers to the benefit of producers when it has them bear the costs of recycling and pollution. It discriminates against patients to the benefit of pharmaceutical companies when it reimburses for certain medications and not for others. It discriminates in news and information when it finances certain media outlets rather than others (and determines what speech is permitted and forbidden). It discriminates between beggars according to whether they are refugees (who are fed, housed, and financially supported) or nationals who have fallen into destitution (who are left out on the street).

The state which arrogates to itself this right to discriminate has in fact a weapon capable of annihilating every individual freedom. This state will soon no longer be under the rule of law.

The democratic state is not accidentally totalitarian; it is *necessarily* totalitarian, for the parties which govern in a democracy can only accede to power and remain there by ever promising and offering more benefits to the bulk of the population. It is inevitably the party which offers the most benefits to the greatest number that has the greatest chance of arriving at and staying in power. Now, in order to be able to offer these benefits to the population, the state must ever become more centralized and more interventionist. It must augment its regulatory powers and thereby reduce individual liberties. It must increase the population's dependence on it, offering ever more services and thus increasing its tax burden. The democratic state is the natural enemy of individual freedom, and of private property which is its guarantee.

If one compares the prerogatives of present-day democratic government with those of the governments of the Ancien Régime or even of most European states in 1900, one is struck by the amount of domains it covers and sectors of activity it controls, subsidizes, and regulates. The democratic state first of all controls the money, whose value and amount in circulation it fixes. It is the arbiter of money production which, thanks to the practice of fractional reserve banking and since the abandonment of the gold standard, is virtually unlimited.[2] It controls public communication services. It controls the supply of energy, from which it derives a good part of its revenue. It controls the news and information outlets, which it subsidizes and regulates. It controls education, which it subsidizes, regulates, and makes compulsory.

The democratic state considerably increased its expenditures and workforce in the course of the twentieth century. Before the First World War, most European governments hardly spent more than ten percent of their GDP. This proportion went up to fifty percent in the 1970s and continues to increase. Similarly, around 1900, public employees almost never represented more than eight percent of the working population. This proportion surpassed fifteen percent in the 1970s and continues to grow.[3] A good number of states multiply their public service positions in order to reduce the unemployment rate, even if the usefulness of these positions is doubtful or altogether lacking. The number of persons dependent on the government directly (civil servants) or indirectly (entitlement recipients) is so great that one can say practically the entire population in a democratic country is dependent on the government for its subsistence. The government in effect subsidizes families, schools, hospitals, welfare programs, housing, a good portion of businesses, and so on, so that it is difficult, even impossible, to progress through

---

[2] See Jörg Guido Hülsmann, *The Ethics of Money Production* (Auburn, AL: Ludwig von Mises Institute, 2008).

[3] Hans-Hermann Hoppe, *Democracy: The God that Failed* (New Brunswick, NJ: Transaction Publishers, 2007), 55-56.

life without having recourse to the intervention of public assistance. Only a tiny minority of the population can avoid this.

Like the Soviet and Nazi totalitarian governments, the democratic state has succeeded in acquiring vast control over the population by making it totally dependent.

Chapter 4

THE WELFARE STATE

THE logical outcome of democracy is the welfare state, that is to say a form of government which feels responsible for its citizens, knows better than they what they need and how to obtain it, and makes provisions in their stead for life's different misfortunes in order to preserve them from them. This image of a state full of solicitude for its citizens was also that which the totalitarian states of the twentieth century projected with a great blaze of propaganda. The reality is that a government which derives its legitimacy, if not its power, from the bulk of its citizens cannot act without disinterest. It would be naive to believe it is charitable or paternally concerned for the good of the people. The government is not a person, but an apparatus. It has no feelings and is not mandated to do charity. Within the apparatus of the government are persons who, due to the characteristic absence of an arbiter in the democratic system, pursue their own personal interests, which rarely coincide with the common good.

In its welfare state dress, the government seeks to make itself indispensable. It does this, so it claims, out of solicitude for the people. It would use its power to come to the aid of the weak, the unfortunate, and the powerless. Now, it is indeed among the functions of government to concern itself with social justice. The first states to establish ministries for social affairs were not parliamentary democracies, but rather the empires of Germany and Austria-Hungary.

However, the monarchs who thus showed a concern for social affairs did so in a true spirit of justice and paternal solicitude, for the sovereign's will was being directly expressed through this government service, and the monarchs had no electoral interest in winning over the citizens of their countries by means of largesse. They were acting as fathers or, at the minimum, as good managers of a family enterprise. This is not the nature of democracies. In democracy, social interventionism is always interested. The objective is to attract voters and, then when the system is up and running, to create a clientele. A democratic state will always act this way because it is in the hands of political parties whose foremost objective is to attain and remain in power.

Will a voter vote for the candidate who promises to help him or for the candidate who tells him he has to fend for himself? He will vote for the one who makes promises in his favor. Thus, democracy is always tending towards interventionism, for the voter is generally egoistic and self-interested, and he will cast his vote for the one who promises to make him the beneficiary of the maximum benefits that the state can offer. The American presidential election of 2008 showed how much weight healthcare reform had in the decision of the voters. It is the reason why President Obama did everything possible to make it pass. The fact that the United States cannot afford the projected costs of this reform is not his concern. The goal of the reform is to assure his popularity among his base. The financial problems will be for his successor.

Individualism is inherent in every democracy. But the welfare state has propelled this tendency to limits not yet explored. Never has a population shown itself so greedy for the enjoyment of state benefits. It insists on maintaining these acquired entitlements, regardless of the consequences for the country as a whole. And in so doing, never has a population surrendered so much of its liberty in order to enjoy these benefits. The welfare state has formed a population that is ever ready to have less liberty in order to have more security, a population of slaves rather than of free men, just as Tocqueville perceived: "They call for equality in freedom; and if they cannot obtain that, they [will] still call for equality in slavery."[1] It was this also that Friedrich Hayek foresaw, for the best slave is the one who desires and loves his chains.[2]

The welfare state concerns itself with the security of the population, with its health, its food, and its leisure. It decides wages, days of leave, work conditions, and pensions. It fixes the amount of taxes, decides interest rates and the value of money. It supplies its population with energy, from which it takes in a considerable profit. It insures its population against unemployment, sickness, old age, and a multitude of other risks. The roles of the welfare state

---

[1] Alexis de Tocqueville, "Why Democratic Nations Show a More Ardent and Enduring Love of Equality Than of Liberty," vol. II, bk. 2, chap. I in *Democracy in America*. Translated by Henry Reeve. (New York: Colonial Press, 1899),
xroads.virginia.edu/~HYPER/DETOC/ch2_01.htm.

[2] See Friedrich Hayek, *The Road to Serfdom* (Abingdon, UK: Routledge, 2003).

are quite numerous, and wherever it aids it also regulates in such a way that the population succumbs to a double dependence, that of the service from which it benefits and that of the regulations to which it must submit.

As a result, the population finds itself at best in a state of assistance, and at worst in a state of parasitism. A population develops very quickly the habit of depending on the government, all the more quickly when it hardly has the choice. It loses thus its vital instincts of foresight, mutual assistance, and family spirit. Its birth rate falls, for the parents no longer need to depend on their progeny to ensure the subsistence and position of the family, nor to assist them in their old age. This population also loses its taste for enterprise and innovation. It loses its spirit of adventure, its natural curiosity, and its singularity. It limits itself in its penchant for security, routine, conformism, and simple pleasures. Such a population becomes individualistic and excessively preoccupied with its own personal problems (such as health and profession) and personal ambitions (such as comfort, food, leisure, and vacation). It becomes small-minded. It gives up its natural defenses and finds itself at the mercy of the least threat, privation, or fear. It counts on the government, even at the price of its liberty.[3]

The welfare state does not only offer its services to its population, but it also imposes them. It does not tolerate declining them. This fundamental right to be able to say no to a government service does not exist

---

[3] See Hilaire Belloc, *The Servile State* (Indianapolis: Liberty Fund, 1977).

in democracy, for whoever would renounce retirement benefits, unemployment benefits, family allowances, free education, and so forth, would still be obliged to contribute to these services through his taxes. The only way, however, to maintain a fair balance of power between the government and the population is to permit the latter to not pay for benefits it does not wish to receive. The people in a welfare state do not have the right to stop paying for public welfare entitlements, even if they renounce their ability to benefit from them. Everyone contributes to free education through taxes, but those who enroll their children in private schools have to pay twice. This remarkable prerogative once again reveals the welfare state's totalitarian face.

Democracy being a system based on opinion, since it is opinion which makes majorities, the major stakes for democratic power are in controlling and influencing opinion. By controlling opinion, it steers the direction of votes and is thus able to remain in power. If the democratic state succeeds in fashioning opinion, it enjoys a solid, lasting, and quasi-unlimited power. It is therefore the inevitable objective of any democracy to fashion and control opinion. For this, it resorts to two principal means: the media and education.

In all democratic states, especially those at an advanced stage in the welfare state system, the government controls the media, whether it owns it, subsidizes it, or controls it by means of a state organ (inevitably always politicized) overseeing radio and television. In all of the countries of Western Europe, the major media outlets are in one form or another under political control. Most of the major dailies and weeklies receive government subsidies, without which, very often, they would go into bankruptcy. The official justification for these subsidies is to enable affordable access to information. The real objective is to control this information in order to form the public's opinion so that it will vote in a certain direction.

The democratic state does the same with education. It makes it free and compulsory so that it is subject to its regulatory powers. In certain countries, like Germany, homeschooling is even prohibited to the point that it is impossible to escape the curricula, teaching methods, and educational values the government wants to impose.[4] Here, again, the justification is social: to make education accessible to all at very low cost. But the real objective is to form the voters of tomorrow by transmitting to them from childhood the thought patterns, values, dos and don'ts one wants them to adopt. "There can be little doubt that compulsory education was an extremely important step towards the totalitarian state."[5]

Through the media and education, the state tries to form the opinion of the voter, for he votes according to his opinion and his vote determines the party (or parties) in power. Thus, the cycle is set and locked. In democracy, the one who controls public opinion controls the reins of power. The fact that there exist several rival parties has little effect on this scheme.

---

[4] The prohibition against homeschooling was adopted by the Nazi government. Federal Germany never gave this freedom back to its people.

[5] Erik von Kuehnelt-Leddihn, *Liberty and Equality* (Front Royal, VA: Christendom Press, 1993), 63.

Nuances of opinion will be permitted, and margins for maneuver will be tolerated. But stray beyond these margins and there are rigorous censures to pressure the nonconformists back into the sheepfold, or at least to isolate and discredit them.

All of the educational systems have deteriorated in both formative quality and content during the past decades. One undoubtedly sees it when comparing the levels of difficulty of mathematical problems and texts imposed on students in 1910, 1950, and today. The decline is catastrophic. It is difficult to refrain from thinking that this is in fact a plan contrived to render the voter less instructed, less critical, more malleable, and more receptive to media propaganda. This fits perfectly with the objective of a government having totalitarian designs. A less critical citizen puts more trust in the state. He is more easily deceived by it. He is slower to defend his autonomy. He is the quintessential "human material" at the state's disposal for consolidating the power and wealth of an oligarchy.

The objective of the state is to have the population accept the social, political, and economic system that it imposes, not as a stopgap, but as the best formula possible. The population conditioned in such a way will spontaneously become disgusted at dissident ideas that the state has designated as enemies of the system in place.

Every state, whatever it may be, defends the principles on which it was founded. The religion, the monarchy, the nation, morality, and property were values which states preceding the welfare state did not compromise. It was not such a long time ago that those considered traitors to the nation were condemned to death. Parliamentary democracy, in its form as a totalitarian-oriented welfare state, makes no exception to this rule. It also has values which cannot be violated, namely anti-racism, anti-fascism, anti-colonialism, anti-classical liberalism, and, more recently, the worrying mental aberrations of anti-discrimination and gender ideology. Democracy, which was born amidst demands for freedom of thought and expression, never itself wanted to tolerate freedom of thought and expression entirely. It persecuted Zola, Marx, and Oscar Wilde, but also Charles Maurras. It forbade fascist parties and monarchical movements, but it has not forbidden communist parties. Democracy does not trust its voters, whom it judges to be immature and in need of safeguards. Democracy, which so forcefully condemned the Index of the Catholic Church, has restored or even never abolished the crime of opinion. Today in the European Union, there are, as in China and Vietnam, dozens of people put into prison for their opinions. Democracy is watching.

In its scheme of social enslavement, the degradation of morals holds a prime place. Its priority target is the family. By stripping the family of its natural role as the basic building block of society, the welfare state has set in motion a process of dissolution, not only of the family itself, but also of the virtues and morals that the family has helped to live and transmit. Divorce, contraception, free unions, abortion, and the lower birth rates mark a rupture with natural and traditional morals. These are deviations resulting from the sabotage of the family as much as they are factors contributing to it. Is this trend by accident? Is this a general evolution independent of the state? It is difficult to believe so, for the democratic state, which banks on claims to individual liberty, has never opposed these trends and, in fact, has supported them. The democratic state, moreover, has been able to exploit this phenomenon.

The family is the bastion of human autonomy and singularity. It is the family which remains the principal organ for the transmission of values, over which the state has no power. The state can control what is said in school or in the media, but it can do nothing about what is said in the family home, at least once the television is turned off. Therefore, it is not unreasonable to see in the current dissolution of morals and the assiduous support democratic states are lending it a fierce and determined war against the family as a natural and Christian institution. The less a human being benefits from the family in the formation of his personality, the more fragile and easily influenced he will be, and the more he will seek the support of the welfare state. He will be the perfect democratic citizen: dependent, malleable, fragile, and without the slightest desire for autonomy.

If one must guard against attributing a single cause to social and moral phenomena, there is also the risk of understanding nothing of these phenomena by drowning them in a multitude of causes. Democracy is the result of a perversion of European thought which manifested itself in the eighteenth century, insofar as it was the goal of a minority that was seeking power. One can say with certainty that it was not, however, the result of a perversion of European society's morals. Democracy came before this perversion. In the beginning of the twentieth century, the family, like professional, social, religious, and national values, was intact, so to speak, in the greater part of society. Democracy, led by a minority seeking its own advantage, has contributed to the dissolution of these values in order to arrive today, under the most advanced form of democracy which is the welfare state, at a marginalization, even almost complete disappearance, of these values.

The welfare state's interventionism is very costly to the taxpayer. It is of no cost to the minister or the parliamentary representative. It is a system which has removed all accountability from the deciders and whose largesse is financed with the money of those who do not decide. The welfare state is, for this reason, inseparable from an ever-increasing tax burden, since the state is always seeking to make itself more indispensable to its citizens. It hastens to offer its services and, in so doing, aggravates the dependence and financial precariousness of its citizens, who, in return, ever seek more protection and benefits from the state.

As the social policy of the welfare state can be justified through arguments of the sentimental kind, opposition to it is not taken well. The one who opposes it is considered selfish and heartless. However, the cost of this policy, which the political class upholds for no other reason than to win elections, must be paid for in one manner or another. The tax burden in a welfare state is inevitably heavy and the infringements on property rights are countless, as are the multiple restrictions imposed on individual freedom by means of the state's regulatory powers. In Belgium, a country whose population is traditionally known for having a well-developed instinct for property, real estate is taxed three times: at its acquisition through registration fees, during its possession through property taxes, and at its transfer through succession fees.

The welfare state is not only costly on account of the services it renders, but also on account of the inevitable waste which accompanies these services. The welfare state is hardly concerned about good budget management, as it has no profit motive and spends public funds not coming from the pockets of the deciders; the fact that there is no independent arbiter, but only an accountability diluted among millions of voters, only contributes to this lack of concern. This neglect inevitably breeds a kind of parasitism and numerous abuses ensue, and the government will only be motivated to correct matters if it can do so without risk to its popularity.

These irresponsible policies are not without dire consequences. The more a population is taxed, the more it is impoverished. With each new onslaught of taxes, the state throws into precariousness a segment of the population that was living modestly, and into misery another segment of the population that was living in precariousness. Given the selective solicitude of democratic states, this levying of taxes, however, does not necessarily or entirely benefit those who are most in need. Thus, during the severely cold weather of the winter of 2012, one could see the Belgian government making a considerable effort to provide decent lodging and assistance to homeless Belgians.

But this same government, whose mania for taxation threw these same people out on the street, offers yearlong housing, assistance, food, and even an integration bonus to immigrants whom the population never invited.

The vicious cycle of the welfare state only stops when the state goes bankrupt, that is to say when the services it offers surpass in cost what the taxpayers are capable of paying. In reality, most democratic states have already passed well beyond this point. But to prolong as much as possible their irresponsible interventionist policies, they have had recourse to borrowing and have massively indebted themselves. It is symptomatic of democracy that the state has the power to indebt its citizens, since a debt incurred by the state is a public debt which the citizens must pay back through their taxes. The breaking point will eventually be reached when the tax burden imposed by the state in order to pay back the public debt becomes too great for the taxpayers to withstand. At that moment, the welfare state will end in chaos and misery, leaving defenseless and without resources a population that was infantilized, because it had become so used to being assisted, and therefore was unable to handle adversity.

But this prospect can still be avoided through repeated recourse to borrowing, so as to continuously inject fresh money into the economy. This does not correct the vices of the welfare state, but it does defer its collapse ... while also aggravating it.

In its 323rd article, the Treaty of Lisbon stipulates that member states of the European Union can no longer borrow money from their central bank, but must borrow exclusively from commercial banks.[6] This requirement only reinforces a practice already in place for several decades. The only difference is that the state must from now on pay interest on amounts borrowed to such an extent that the public debt of certain states is comprised more of interest than of principal. In all other respects, the operation is the same. Whether it is the central bank or the commercial banks injecting money into the economy, it is a matter in both cases of "fiat money," meaning money created at the moment of the loan and not in any way backed by a reserve. The commercial banks practice the system of fractional reserve banking, and are thus legally authorized to lend much more than they hold in deposit. This well-known quasi-unlimited expansion of credit, rightly denounced by the Austrian school of economics,[7] is the only way to finance the welfare state on a long-term basis.

This mode of financing, then, must be understood as the fruit of collaboration between the democratic state and the banks. Each of the two partners benefits from this: the banks, by receiving interest on the money they are authorized to create, and the state, by reducing the population to a state of dependence through its largesse and its regulations. It must be noted that the population is, at any rate, losing out, for what they believe to be gaining from the state's generosity, they lose in individual freedom and in purchasing power. Indeed, the population of a welfare

---

[6] Note the ability of financial institutions to dictate the contents of treaties.

[7] For more on this subject, see Jörg Guido Hülsmann, *The Ethics of Money Production* (Auburn, AL: Ludwig von Mises Institute, 2008).

state becomes irreparably poorer due to the inflation provoked by the state and the banks. It does not even have the freedom to safeguard its purchasing power by abandoning the use of a currency which is continuously losing its value in exchange for something more stable, for the currency is legal tender which no one is permitted to refuse as payment. Thus, the state holds in its hands the wealth of the population, especially of the middle class, which does not have the ability to invest abroad or to break loose somehow from the shackles of state control.

At the moment of this writing, the European Central Bank has just injected more than one trillion euros into the economy of the eurozone in the form of one percent interest rate loans allotted to approximately eight hundred banks. This new expansion of the money supply only increases the uncertainty about the unique currency's viability. It portends a new upsurge in inflation. It sends a conflicting message to the eurozone states, which are on the one hand asked to reduce their expenses, and on the other hand assured of being bailed out if they spend too much.

The case of Greece is symptomatic of a welfare state that has used up all of its options. With a deficient tax system and a population composed largely of public assistance recipients, the governments secured power for themselves through social largesse for which they did not have the means. They therefore recklessly indebted the state until it became obvious the debts could not be paid back without foreign aid. This aid was granted, to the greatest benefit of the banks, and in order to maintain the credibility of the eurozone. But at no moment did this crisis prompt a serious reflection on the future of the welfare state or on the pernicious effects of credit expansion due to the fractional reserve system. The state and the banks, responsible for the chaos, take great care not to put their monopoly in danger. Other countries will follow, and ideology and greed will be forced to come to terms with reality.

For this crisis, there are only two possible outcomes. Either the state cuts its spending and ceases providing assistance to the population (and in so doing gives up its regulatory arsenal), or it continues on the path of currency production in order to sustain the imposed social system. In the second case, the state is going to trigger hyperinflation, which will destroy the population's purchasing power and lead to an economic disaster similar or even worse than the one Germany experienced after the First World War.

In the case of a reform of the welfare state occurring through a drastic reduction in spending, one must expect a revolution, for the population will not accept sinking into misery for the sole reason that bankers and politicians sought power and riches in the most irresponsible manner. In both cases, one must expect an indescribable chaos to result from the collapse of the current system.

It is necessary to add that this extreme was reached because the state abusively deprived the population of its rightful freedoms. If the banks had been bound to a total reserve system, that is to say all loans had been guaranteed by precious metal reserves and at any moment paper currency could have been exchanged for this precious metal, credit would have never undergone such an expansion, the banks would have never acquired so much power, the state would have been forced to watch its spending, and the specter of hyperinflation would have never shown itself. But the state preferred to please the banks without any regard for the common good.

The welfare state, a fruit of democracy, is an entirely new phenomenon in the history of political systems. It was, however, foreseen and described by Alexis de Tocqueville in 1840, in a passage striking for its accuracy:

> I think, then, that the species of oppression by which democratic nations are menaced is unlike anything that ever before existed in the world; our contemporaries will find no prototype of it in their memories. I seek in vain for an expression that will accurately convey the whole of the idea I have formed of it; the old words despotism and tyranny are inappropriate: the thing itself is new, and since I cannot name, I must attempt to define it.
>
> I seek to trace the novel features under which despotism may appear in the world. The first thing that strikes the observation is an innumerable multitude of men, all equal and alike, incessantly endeavoring to procure the petty and paltry pleasures with which they glut their lives. Each of them, living apart, is as a stranger to the fate of all the rest; his children and his private friends constitute to him the whole of mankind. As for the rest of his fellow citizens, he is close to them, but he does not see them; he touches them, but he does not feel them; he exists only in himself and for himself alone; and if his kindred still remain to him, he may be said at any rate to have lost his country.
>
> Above this race of men stands an immense and tutelary power, which takes upon itself alone to secure their gratifications and to watch over their fate. That power is absolute, minute, regular, provident, and mild.

It would be like the authority of a parent if, like that authority, its object was to prepare men for manhood; but it seeks, on the contrary, to keep them in perpetual childhood: it is well content that the people should rejoice, provided they think of nothing but rejoicing. For their happiness such a government willingly labors, but it chooses to be the sole agent and the only arbiter of that happiness; it provides for their security, foresees and supplies their necessities, facilitates their pleasures, manages their principal concerns, directs their industry, regulates the descent of property, and subdivides their inheritances: what remains, but to spare them all the care of thinking and all the trouble of living?

Thus it every day renders the exercise of the free agency of man less useful and less frequent; it circumscribes the will within a narrower range and gradually robs a man of all the uses of himself. The principle of equality has prepared men for these things; it has predisposed men to endure them and often to look on them as benefits.

After having thus successively taken each member of the community in its powerful grasp and fashioned him at will, the supreme power then extends its arm over the whole community. It covers the surface of society with a network of small complicated rules, minute and uniform, through which the most original minds and the most energetic characters cannot penetrate, to rise above the crowd. The will of man is not shattered, but softened, bent, and guided; men are seldom forced by it to act, but they are constantly restrained from acting. Such a power does not destroy, but it prevents existence; it does not tyrannize, but it compresses, enervates, extinguishes, and stupefies a people, till each nation is reduced to nothing better than a flock of timid and industrious animals, of which the government is the shepherd.[8]

---

[8] Alexis de Tocqueville, "What Sort of Despotism Democratic Nations Have to Fear," vol. II, bk. 4, chap. VI in *Democracy in America*. Translated by Henry Reeve. (New York: Colonial Press, 1899), xroads.virginia.edu/~HYPER/DETOC/ch4_06.htm.

Chapter 5

THE EUROPEAN UNION

The totalitarian orientation of democracy is easily observed in every democratic nation-state. Everywhere it is the same unbridled growth in the prerogatives of the state, in its power to regulate, to intervene, and to discriminate. Everywhere there is also the same unaccountability and the same corruption among the ruling oligarchy. The European Union is not exempt from this same orientation. It is an excellent example of a transnational superstructure meant to serve foreign interests at the expense of the populations it administers. But of course democratic forms are preserved in order to maintain the populations in delusion. In practice, the European Union reproduces the same defects found in national governments, but what gives it more of an exemplary character is that it reproduces these defects exponentially. The distance it puts between itself and the European populations makes its totalitarian dysfunction more flagrant and its effects more visible.

This chapter is a somewhat revised version of an essay originally published in Dutch as "De totalitaire dynamiek van de Europese Unie," in *Europa wankelt: De ontvoering van Europa door de EU*, ed. Wim van Rooy, Remi Hauman, and Sam van Rooy (Kessel-Lo, Belgium: Van Halewyck, 2012), 296-315. The financial numbers mentioned in this chapter date from the time of original publication in 2012.

Its examination is therefore most useful for showing the true nature of a democratic system.

What should sound the alarm is that the European Union is always seeking to justify its own existence. Being a superstructure rather than a nation-state, it feels the need to explain why it is so indispensable. A nation-state does not feel this need to justify itself, for it has a basis in the people and there is a general consensus favoring its existence which it can afford to take for granted. But the European Union cannot claim these advantages. Thus, it must find other grounds on which to establish its legitimacy.

The European Union made the Franco-German reconciliation its dominant theme. It has used this moral justification to make appear as normal the concentration of power from which it benefits at the expense of member states' sovereignty. This reconciliation also justifies the seat of the European Parliament in Strasbourg, which is a considerable source of useless spending. The argument of peace stemming from the Franco-German reconciliation is also rehashed at every opportunity. The European Union has supposedly brought sixty years of peace to Europe. This self-awarded commendation is all the more remarkable considering Western Europe has not experienced any threat of an internal war throughout this period and, consequently, no war was able to be avoided on account of the European Union. Furthermore, even if such a threat had existed, one can hardly imagine how the European Union would have been able to do anything to resolve it. It is, after all, militarily impotent and diplomatically divided— qualities that appear to be present in one form or another in every conflict that erupts in the world. The idea that NATO was responsible for securing peace in Western Europe is a completely defendable notion, but to argue the same for the European Union is utterly ridiculous.

The European Union seeks a justification to give to its citizens. If it is not peace, then it would allegedly be the euro. The majority of Europeans consider the single currency to be what makes them undoubtedly the most grateful for the European Union. Certainly, they are not yet taking into account the negative aspects associated with the euro's introduction— inflation, the lack of flexibility during a time of crisis, the loss of national sovereignty, and the risk of the eurozone's collapse—but most of all they lose sight of the fact that the European Union was never *necessary* for a single currency. Charlemagne himself also imposed a single currency within his empire without having had need for an exorbitantly massive administration and a weighty and costly infrastructure such as belong to the European Union. The single currency—the (near?) future will tell us if this has truly contributed to the prosperity of Europeans— could have resulted from an intergovernmental agreement between sovereign states, such as occurred with the Belgium-Luxembourg monetary union; and the establishment of the European Central Bank did not require a commission, a parliament, and the entire bureaucratic apparatus of the European Union.

The question of knowing whether the European Union serves the interests of Europeans must not be obfuscated by these pretenses of Eurocratic propaganda. No, Europeans do not owe peace in

Western Europe to the European Union. And no, advantages such as a single currency and free movement between countries do not necessitate the European Union's concentration of power.

The only question that must be asked is this one: Has the European Union contributed to the good of Europeans in ways that the national governments were incapable of doing? Or rather: Does the European Union capitalize on its supranational standing in order to efficiently and effectively serve the good of Europeans? Seen from this vantage point, the European Union already appears much less convincing. Europeans do not have the impression it contributes in a decisive manner to either their prosperity or their security. They cannot thank it for effectively defending their borders from immigration, or the European market from Asian competition. They do not have it to thank for any administrative simplifications or any tax relief, quite the contrary. And they cannot thank it for its military presence since it has no army to speak of. These are all the areas where the European Union ought to be distinguishing itself, but nothing of consequence is to be seen. One would even tend to say that the European Union aggravates matters, and that each time it is found at fault it tends to deflect responsibility onto the member states.

The European Union is an excellent testing ground for the oligarchic orientation proper to every democratic system. The relative proximity that exists between the citizens and the state in nation-states can act as a check to this orientation, for its political class is constantly under the critical eye of the voters, even if the latter are powerless and misinformed. This safeguard vanishes in the European Union. The distance is too great between the population and the elite of the Eurocracy. First of all, one must not forget that, for the overwhelming majority of Europeans, Brussels is in a foreign land. This reinforces the extraneous, even illegitimate, character of decisions made by the European Union. Secondly, since Europeans are already considerably preoccupied following their national politics and are not so interested in European politics, national affairs act as a kind of smokescreen. Lastly, the European Union, on account of its very structure, its complexity, and its lack of transparency, is cut off from the European population. Despite its protestations to the contrary, the EU seeks this distance, which gives it free hands and increases its power.

As with any political system lacking an independent arbiter—something that is a distinctive feature of democracy—the European Union brings together the two most common forms of corruption. The first is generally the only one that is considered as such: it is the corruption of the deciders by external agents seeking decisions in their favor. The European Union is subject to this form of corruption on a very large scale. One might remember the case of European Commission President José Manuel Barroso, who spent his vacation on the yacht of Greek billionaire Spiro Latsis shortly before the European Commission approved 10 million euros in Greek state aid to the ship-owner's company. Even if the affair did fizzle out, many continue to regard it as a case of corruption.

The "phony lobbyists" affair is also worth recalling. The apparent lobbyists were in reality journalists from the *Sunday Times*. They succeeded in filing amendments via three European Parliament members (MEPs) who made their services available in exchange for cash. The three elected officials implicated were Adrian Severin, the former Romanian Deputy Prime Minister, Zoran Thaler, the former Slovenian Minister of Foreign Affairs, and Ernst Strasser, the former Austrian Minister of the Interior. The British reporters confirmed recognizing the text they had proposed for inclusion in an EU consumer protection bill. The corrupt delegates each gave instructions to the phony lobbyists concerning the bank or company where they should deposit the money. According to the *Sunday Times*, Adrian Severin sent an email to the journalists saying, "Just to let you know that the amendment desired by you has been tabled in due time."[1] Shortly thereafter, he sent a bill in the amount of 12,000 euros for "consulting services." Zoran Thaler himself also put forward an amendment, asking afterwards that the money for him be deposited into the account of a company in London. The third delegate, Ernst Strasser, introduced a draft amendment via colleagues sitting on a committee and asked for an initial deposit of 25,000 euros into the account of a company he owned in Austria. The total cost of the corruption scheme would have amounted to about 100,000 euros if everything had proceeded as planned.

---

[1] Jonathan Calvert, Claire Newell, and Michael Gillard, "Euro MPs Exposed in 'Cash-for-Laws' Scandal," *Sunday Times* (London), March 20, 2011.

Jerzy Buzek, the President of the European Parliament at the time of these events, authorized the European Anti-Fraud Office (OLAF) to investigate the bribed delegates. At the same time, however, he denied it access to the parliamentarians' offices. This is because the European Parliament feared other unseemly matters would come to light,[2] even if the risk were slight given that OLAF is itself an organ of the Eurocratic apparatus and therefore potentially corrupt as well. One might remember that already in 2008, one of the most influential German officials in the European Commission, Fritz-Harald Wenig, had been forced to resign after an investigation by the *Sunday Times*[3] was carried out according to the same method of journalists posing as bribing lobbyists. In 2004, the Greek official, Kalliopi Nikolaou, a member of the European Court of Auditors in Luxembourg, allegedly purchased a London apartment with money from unjustified bonus payments. And in 1999, French Research Commissioner Edith Cresson gave a close friend a fictitious job that was financed with European funds—a scandal that led to the collective resignation of the Santer Commission. Corruption is evidently a fact of daily life in the European Union, and what has come to light is undoubtedly just the tip of the iceberg.

If this form of corruption is the only one that appears to normally be limited, that is because it is illegal. It therefore always runs the risk of being

---

[2] And for good reason! If journalists posing as lobbyists can successfully bribe European delegates, how many more corruption cases ought we to expect with the thousands of genuine lobbyists who besiege the European Parliament on a daily basis?

[3] September 7, 2008.

exposed and punished—even if such an eventuality is apparently rare enough and not particularly painful.

The other form of corruption, called *internal* or *institutional* corruption, originates inside the institution itself and according to norms deemed acceptable by the institution. There was a lot of talk when MEPs voted to increase the monthly budget allotted them for paying their assistants' salaries— they voted for an additional 1,500 euros per month when there was already 19,709 euros allocated monthly for this purpose. This budget is in addition to the individual MEP monthly salary of 7,956.87 euros, which is further augmented by multiple supplements here and there. Europeans who heard about the voted budget increase did not receive the news particularly well, as it occurred at the very same time that national governments were being called on by the European Union and others to cut their spending.

Wealth, and in particular sudden financial affluence, has a disastrous effect on the morality of its beneficiaries. And among the disorders observed, the most flagrant is the loss of the sense of reality. Very quickly, the newly enriched person comes to believe he deserves his salary—and even that he deserves more than his salary. He ceases to see poverty or the financial difficulties of those around him. He thinks of himself as the norm and sees nothing excessive, scandalous, or unjust in making ten times more than certain modest workers. This transformation can happen very quickly. It is all the more so when the beneficiary is a public civil servant who can deflect on the state or the European Union responsibility for the abuses from which he profits. He is unable to justify the thousands of euros that pour into his bank account each month: he cannot justify it by his workload, which is not particularly heavy; nor by his obligation to achieve results, which is actually rather limited; nor by his merit, which often consists merely in happening to know the right people; nor by his production of wealth, which is zero. This unjustified wealth, however, does not keep him from sleeping at night. The first instinct of this civil servant is to cut himself off from the real world. The European civil servant is one who mostly moves about in closed circles. He seeks his own kind, for to them he does not have to justify his income or his privileges. With them, evidence of an excessive and unjustifiable salary is not constantly put before him. He ends up believing his situation is normal, and even that it is due him, for man is, by nature, full of himself.

The institution that corrupts its employees this way, both morally and monetarily, knows very well what it is doing. In spite of the blinders worn by the civil servant in his everyday life, he knows full well he owes his golden situation to the institution that pays him. Thus, he is naturally inclined to behave in a way that enables him to keep his situation and to even improve it, if possible. He will seek to please the institution and be very careful not to contradict or criticize it, even if he should see legitimate reasons for doing so. He will silence his conscience and find good reasons to cover up the abuses he witnesses. This is the behavior expected of European civil servants, and it is for this reason they are excessively well paid and enjoy numerous privileges.

The Soviet Union, which resembles the European Union in many respects, practiced this same type of internal corruption. Its civil servants were members of the Communist Party. They had the privilege of being paid in foreign currency and, as a result, could make their purchases in stores reserved exclusively for tourists and Communist Party members which sold goods unavailable to the rest of the population. Members of the Communist Party also enjoyed numerous privileges which set them apart from the rest of the citizenry. They managed to convince themselves easily enough that the system was just— after all, anyone could become a Communist Party member.

In the case of the European Union, internal corruption is not limited to civil servants, but it extends as well to MEPs, all kinds of offices for research and publishing, and a large number of lobbying organizations that the European Union subsidizes. Is it necessary to recall that all of this is done with public funds? The European Union itself decides its own spending and budget increases. It shows itself very hostile to independent auditors and normally throws their reports into the trash.[4] The European Union itself appoints the director of OLAF, whose zeal it knows how to temper should the latter forget the rules of the game.

---

[4] Let us recall here the misadventure of Chief Accountant Maria Andreasen, who refused to sign off on the accounts for the year 2001 since they entailed an astounding margin of error of 5 billion euros. Her personal investigation led her to subsequently conclude that the actual margin of error was close to 15 billion euros. She was suspended in May 2002. The accounts of the European Union have not been approved properly since 1996 (*Brussels Journal*, January 21, 2010).

Driven by the ever sufficient motive of money, the European Union indulges itself in numerous contortions of its own institutional rules, not to mention basic principles of justice; it stews in massive waste, blatant manifestations of incompetence, fraudulent practices, and even violations of what it purports to consider sacred: democracy and human rights.

In a special edition, the French magazine *Le Cri du Contribuable* published "Europe's Black Book," the introduction of which reads:

> The Treaty of Lisbon—in force since December 1st following the Irish yes vote and the Czech ratification—expands Brussels' powers to sixty-eight new fields of jurisdiction, enshrines the absolute superiority of European laws over national laws, and makes the European Union a quasi-state, endowed with juridical personality, a Council President, and a Super-Ministry of Foreign Affairs. At the risk of aggravating its bad behavior, 95% of the communal budget is consecrated to "super-welfare state" programs. For close to fifteen years, the European Court of Auditors has issued an unfavorable ruling on 80% of these expenditures, which it has judged to be illegal or irregular. These expenditures, in the hands of the European Commission, are bound up between it and a clientele to which it is obligated, to the detriment of the paying states, and of, therefore, the taxpayers.[5]

In other words, the European Union is the premier organ of European subsidizing by volume of money

---

[5] Benoîte Taffin and Laurent Artur du Plessis, eds., "Le Livre noir de l'Europe: 80 scandales concrets," *Le Cri du Contribuable*, special issue no. 1 (December 2009).

distributed. We cannot take up here all eighty scandals laid into by *Le Cri du Contribuable*, but neither can we resist the (dis)pleasure of mentioning some of these expenditures, all the more lavish because other people's money paid for them:

• Salaries. The annual salary of a European commissioner is €238,219 and that of the President of the European Commission, currently José Manuel Barroso, is up at €293,073. In addition to this, there is a housing allowance of €43,960 and a representation allowance of €17,017. Thus, the total salary for the President of the European Commission is €354,050 per year, meaning €29,504 per month, and, if he works a 35-hour week, €210 per hour. The President of the European Commission therefore makes more than European heads of state and even more than the President of the United States. The Minister of Foreign Affairs, Catherine Ashton, despite her manifest incompetence and the uselessness of her position, makes €363,000 per year. Upon leaving her post, she will enjoy a pension of €70,439 per year and a departure bonus of €510,500. The President of the European Council, Herman Van Rompuy, makes about the same. The MEPs are not poorly served either: despite the reigning confusion about the numbers, it can be established that an MEP takes in close to €9,000 per month in salary and attendance fees, to which is added an annual general expense allowance of €4,202 and a travel allowance of €4,148. It should also be pointed out that an MEP is not held to any results requirements and need not demonstrate any particular competencies.

• Subsidies. The most striking case is that of Turkey, which receives a "pre-accession" subsidy of 564 million euros annually to assist it in financing the internal reforms necessary for entrance into the European Union. This aid is expected to increase each year though several European heads of state are firmly opposed to Turkish membership and 70% of Europeans reject it. Subsidies are what figure most prominently in the budget of the Eurocracy. The European Union subsidizes everything and anything, from agrifood giants to marionette theatres, from electoral campaigns to hotel chains, from golf courses to even lobbying organizations that are supposed to defend their interests in complete independence.

• Waste. Here we address the Eurocracy's wasteful spending at its apex. The best example is the European Parliament, which is "required" to hold twelve monthly plenary sessions per year in Strasbourg, some 440 kilometers (273 miles) from the MEPs' main offices in Brussels. Each month, 785 European representatives, their assistants, and a large portion of the administration move, as well as six semitrailers full of files along with them. The costs of these twelve moves and the upkeep of the buildings in Strasbourg during the rest of the year amount to 250 million euros annually. In a single parliamentary term, this accounts for 1.25 billion euros in spending. The seat of the European Parliament is maintained in Strasbourg at the sole request of the French, out of chauvinism, and of some German representatives who happen to live nearby. Note that this cost represents close to half of the budget allocated for modernizing

Turkey according to European standards. This means that if the seat in Strasbourg were suppressed, the European Union could, without any budget increase, assist a European country smaller or less backward than Turkey in meeting European standards.

- Propaganda. Like any other totalitarian apparatus, the European Union is quick to set aside a portion of its budget for the purpose of convincing voters of its benefits. Thus, in an effort to curb voter abstentionism in the June 2009 European elections, it approved a budget of 15.4 million euros for this purpose. The participation rate ended up being 43%, which was a total failure. The 40 million euro investment in Europarl TV, the channel of the European Parliament, also similarly failed. On the other hand, the European Union invested 1.8 million euros to obtain the Irish yes vote in the country's second referendum. Violating the law on referendum campaign financing, the European Union had guides favoring the Treaty of Lisbon inserted into all of the Irish newspapers the Sunday preceding the vote—the cost of this operation was 150,000 euros. At least, in this case, the effort succeeded—the European Union "triumphed" over Irish skepticism.

The European Union has long understood the game it must play to further its agenda. It seeks to "clientelize" Europe in order to justify its power and its spending. It first begins by guaranteeing itself the total submission of its personnel by means of extravagant salaries. It is essential that these personnel have an uncompromised sense of obligation to the

European Union and that they genuinely feel they would be nothing without it. These personnel will therefore show themselves to be totally accommodating and will close their eyes to all kinds of irregularities, fraud, abuse, and injustice. The simple fact of living in the artificial and privileged world of the European Union will suffice to cut them off from the realities of society and prepare them to accept as normal the oligarchic and anti-democratic orientation of the institutions. Next, it seeks to draw the peoples to itself through a panoply of wide-ranging subsidies. But is it possible to draw in entire peoples simply through money? The European Union's practice of large-scale corruption, both internal and external, serves only to keep a rotten edifice standing. The European Union only exists to dole out benefits and is supported by those who benefit from them.

If the European budget deficit is worrying,[6] there is another kind of deficit that ought to preoccupy Europeans, what is commonly called the "democratic deficit."[7] The European Union is oriented towards oligarchy and is built on a privileged elite that is becoming more and more exclusive. It is unlikely Robert Schuman had in mind to put in place a European Commission that was unelected, unaccountable, and highly privileged. He perhaps did not imagine either that a European Parliament having no direct right of legislative initiative would itself also be heavily privileged, imposing fines on its own

---

[6] There was a deficit of 550 million euros in payments in the 2011 European Union budget. *Europolitics*, October 21, 2011.

[7] This is an inapt expression. One ought to say "representation deficit."

members when they stray into politically incorrect discourse. All of this has been pointed out as an unnatural deviation by the European voter, as well as by some all too rare but courageous MEPs.

In reality, this is not at all an unnatural deviation, since this is precisely the natural and universally observed development in parliamentary democracy. As democracy is both a system of government and a system of representation, when one speaks of a democratic deficit, one really means parliamentary representation is no longer working. This phenomenon can be observed in all national democracies and explains the growing interest in direct democracy and referenda, such as practiced in Switzerland. But, as a system of government, democracy works very well, so much so that the representative system is even absorbed and neutralized. It is no longer the voters who are represented, but the political parties and the lobbies. The influence of the latter on the European Parliament is so powerful that it would be more economical to seat them in the place of the elected representatives. One would undoubtedly get the same results.

This reduction of parliamentary democracy to only one of its two roles is not an unnatural evolution. The power in a democracy naturally tends to concentrate around its organized elite. The European Union illustrates perfectly this phenomenon and amazingly calls to mind the Soviet Union, as the famous Russian dissident Vladimir Bukovsky has himself pointed out.[8]

---

[8] See Vladimir Boukovsky and Pavel Stroilov, *L'Union européenne, une nouvelle URSS ?*, trans. Pierre Lorrain (Monaco: Le Rocher, 2005).

The Soviet Union was run by fifteen individuals, who were unelected, unaccountable, and unable to be removed from their positions. The Soviet Union also had a parliament, the Supreme Soviet, which lacked the right of legislative initiative, had a limited freedom of expression, and was responsible for approving the decisions of the Politburo. The Soviet Union was also administered by thousands of civil servants showered with privileges and belonging to the Communist Party. Now it is in this, one might say, that the European Union fundamentally differs from the Soviet Union, since there is no single party. But this is only true in appearance. The European Union has no single party because it does not need one. To preserve power in sure hands, it suffices for it to have a single political class and an army of civil servants made servile through corruption. Beyond the sufficiently negligible ideological differences among the major political groups of the European Parliament, there exists a large basis of consensus upon which the Commission is able to build a stable power. The reality of the single party is replaced by that of the privileged political class, whose members are reinstituted by recommendation or cooptation and selected according to their ideological allegiance to the Eurocratic project.[9]

The European Union, one might still insist, does not have a state police or a gulag. This is true enough. But if the European Union has not put in place a police system like the Soviet Union or the Nazi government, this is again because it is not necessary. Opposition is

---

[9] The member states do not even have full liberty in the appointment of the European commissioners, as was demonstrated by the unsuccessful candidacy of Rocco Buttiglione.

certainly growing in Europe, but it has not yet represented a vital threat to the European Union. Control of the European Union population is not exercised through terror or intimidation. It operates by means of education, the media, and subsidies. It also counts on the progressive impoverishment of the middle class, which is too busy trying to get by financially and cannot afford to get involved in politics. If, by chance, a popular leader should pose a real threat to the Establishment, someone such as a Pim Fortuyn or a Jörg Haider,[10] then there is always the option of assassination...

The European Union thus appears to be a well-oiled machine designed to control the European peoples, a kind of soft version of the classic totalitarian state known in the twentieth century. Its real objective, aside from the enrichment of its members, is to serve as machinery in the grand scheme of global governance. The European Union is not at the service of Europeans.

This basic fact should not be a surprise to anyone since the ratification of the Treaty of Lisbon. Recall that the European Constitution project was officially abandoned following the negative referenda in France and the Netherlands. But the Eurocracy had not had their last word. It recast the essential elements of the European Constitution in a new treaty—the Treaty of Lisbon—which enabled the European Union to

---

[10] Pim Fortuyn of the Netherlands and Jörg Haider of Austria were both populist party leaders gaining in political influence at the time of their sudden deaths. Fortuyn was assassinated by a gunman just nine days before the 2002 Dutch general election. As for Haider, he was killed less than two weeks after the 2008 Austrian legislative election in what was officially ruled a mere car accident but which some theorize was foul play.—Trans.

become a superstate without proclaiming it too loudly. Ireland put its own ratification of the treaty to a referendum as required by its constitution and it was rejected by a majority vote in 2008. This setback for the European Union was attributed to interference by groups of influence outside the control of the Irish political parties, in other words to the free initiative of private society. As giving up on the Treaty of Lisbon was out of the question, the European Union forced a new referendum in 2009 and, this time, ensured there would be propaganda in place favoring a yes vote. The official line of thought was that no one says no to the European Union unless it is because they have not understood the issue well; and that when they do understand it well, they inevitably say yes. It is astounding that so many reputedly intelligent and educated people have bought into this crudely simplistic narrative. In the second referendum, whether they were tired of it all or they were simply misled, the Irish people delivered a majority yes vote.

This forcing of the Treaty of Lisbon shows us two things: that the European Union has nothing but contempt for people's opinions, even when they constitute the majority, and that it nevertheless wants to preserve the outward appearance of democracy.

The contempt for the opinion of Europeans can still be seen in the question of Turkey's entrance into the European Union. There has been no referendum on this issue but polling shows 60% to 70% of Europeans are against Turkey's admission into the Union.[11] This is inversely proportional to the political class, where

---

[11] French Institute of Public Opinion poll, September 4, 2008.

an overwhelming majority express being in favor of this Asian country's entrance. Despite the opposition of the European population, which, in a democracy, ought to prevail, the European Union has constantly reaffirmed its determination to pursue the negotiations and financing for pre-accession. Proof that Turkey's accession is unpopular was furnished by Nicolas Sarkozy, who made the rejection of Turkish candidacy one of the themes of his campaign in the presidential elections. But he also gave proof of his duplicity and his submission to other interests when, holding the rotating presidency of the Council of the European Union, he pursued negotiations with Turkey, as well as funding for its pre-accession.

These particular refusals to respect the will of the people, not to mention many others, reveal that the European Union answers to its own agenda, which must be accomplished regardless of the population's opposition. This is characteristic of a totalitarian state. The Soviet Union also asserted it was "true democracy" and boasted it was genuinely at the population's service. The absurdity of this claim was obvious to many people, even inside the Soviet Union, but that did not prevent the regime from holding together for seventy years.

As a nexus of regional power, the European Union has no concern for popular opinion. It is at the service of more dominant forces and their financial and strategic interests. Its role stops there.

Chapter 6

LEFT AND RIGHT

T HE greatest misunderstanding about democracy is perhaps that concerning the alternation between left and right. Any observer should realize just how pointless this swinging of the political pendulum is for the common good and also just how misleading it is regarding representation. Democracy has come to a point where the voters no longer vote *for* a candidate but rather *against* his opponent. Generally, an opposition candidate is voted for when the president or the party in power has amassed sufficient reasons for dissatisfaction and disappointment among the voters. The actual merits of the candidate, inasmuch as they exist, are unknown most of the time and have nothing to do with his being elected.

Thus, Obama was elected President because Americans had had enough of Bush. And similarly, Sarkozy, when he had begun to tire the French, fell to Hollande, who was fortunate enough to be the candidate on the left at that particular moment.

This pendulum swinging, or democratic alternation, has nothing then to do with representation. A candidate's victory is due to his media image (which also depends on the image of his opponent), his financial means,[1] and the humor of the electorate at

---

[1] The 2016 U.S. presidential election once again showed how important financial means are in running a campaign.

111

that particular moment. Two months later, it is possible that the same electorate, without any apparent reason, would vote differently. It is often the case that the popularity of an elected government declines soon after it has assumed power, which clearly shows how much this popularity is based solely on words and images. After reality hits, popularity quickly dwindles.

Democratic alternation, moreover, is ruinous to the common good. A legislature busies itself enacting laws on ideological grounds or even to increase its popularity. The pernicious effects of these laws will not be felt until the following legislative term. Each government, each presidency, each administration, faced with the uncertainty of not having their power renewed, has the tendency to empty the state coffers and to enrich their party, leaving to the opposition the task of managing the deficit thus created. Democracy, instead of encouraging foresight and frugality, institutionalizes recklessness and waste.

In democracy, the voters are forever dissatisfied and the campaign theme of change resonates very well, whereas the theme of continuity is rarely invoked. This is paradoxical since the population supposedly already has a government according to their wishes. But successive governments, not serving the common good, generate a profound dissatisfaction which only serves to favor the left-right alternation.[2]

What might escape the attention of the political observer, however, is that the left always has a better

---

[2] The left-right alternation poses no difficulty for the money powers as long as their interests are unharmed. In fact, it even works to their benefit, for they can promise support to the more docile party and penalize the party that defies them.

chance than the right of getting elected. The left is naturally better situated to engage in demagogic discourse. It is the left that wants to indulge the population, to be generous and helpful, and to assist them in their difficulties. The right, in principle, promises liberty, which implies personal responsibility, risk, and inequalities. That man would be ready to pay this price for liberty is not a sure thing. Faced with a choice between the security promised by the left and the liberty promised by the right, the majority of the population will choose security. Liberty is a noble value that does not appeal to the desires of everyone, and democracy is a system of the masses.

The voter might vote to the right most of the time during periods of general well-being or high economic growth, or even in circumstances which arouse a sense of patriotism. But the morosity of ordinary democratic life prompts him to vote leftward more often, especially if the future is dark and thoughts of his own personal situation inspire in him sentiments of bitterness and depression.

Thus, by its very nature, democracy drifts to the left. In a masterful work,[3] Eric von Kuehnelt-Leddihn showed how parliamentary democracy is essentially a phenomenon of the left. It will always gravitate towards more government, more interventionism, more taxation, and less individual and collective liberty. Periods of remission will exist, of course, and

---

[3] Erik von Kuehnelt-Leddihn, *Leftism Revisited: From de Sade and Marx to Hitler and Pol Pot* (Washington, DC: Regnery, 1990).

prosperity can still abound in democracy, but its overall movement will be towards the left.

Proponents of classical liberal democracy were only democrats because they believed democracy could be continuously maintained on the right. But since the advent of universal suffrage, that is no longer possible. Power, in a democracy, is only earned by promising to please the majority of the voters, and it is the candidate promising the most gifts who will receive the majority of the votes. The fact that his promises are not kept or that once fulfilled they beget a yet more serious situation can bring the voters back to the right for a time. But the voters forget very quickly. There is no collective memory in a culture dominated by the media. The left will always end up returning to power, regardless of their lies and betrayals.[4]

This is so true that the right imitates this behavior. In order not to be permanently excluded from power, the right has itself moved to the left. It has adopted most of the left's themes so that the parties in Europe today called "conservative" have little in common with their pre-war ancestors. They even go so far as to disown them. The left and right today are in fact merely two aspects of the same political current. Their styles vary, and so do their voting constituencies. The degrees of leftism can be different, but the fundamental principles are the same. Their differences are more of a sociological rather than ideological order.

---

[4] Emmanuel Macron's election to the French presidency in 2017 is an enlightening demonstration of this fact.

Whether they are on the left or on the right, the main European political parties are in agreement on what is essential in their eyes: a government that is powerful, interventionist, and as centralized as possible; a privileged political class enjoying a certain immunity and open to corruption; equality before the law (but not so much in the practical order); the politicization of the media, the civil service, the justice system and the military; subjecting political decisions to the interests of the money powers—therefore globalism and immigration; rejecting all fascism (especially corporatism) and all nationalism (except in times of crisis in order to galvanize the masses); rejecting all traditional morality while unconditionally defending a state morality based on human rights, secularism, relativism, and anti-discrimination; the necessity of a central bank, unlimited credit (thus rejection of the gold standard), and inflation; parliamentary representation, upheld as the only system of representation; rejecting the referendum, or being extremely skeptical of it, as of any form of direct democracy; heavy taxation; free and compulsory education; omnipresent bureaucracy and state interventionism in as many domains as possible. Lastly, all democratic parties condemn anything reminiscent, even remotely, of the Ancien Régime, such as monarchy, nobility,[5] an inegalitarian and complementary society, customary law,

---

[5] Rare are the democratic governments, such as those of the United Kingdom and Belgium, which still confer titles of nobility. It is remarkable that socialist politicians who have worked all their lives for a classless society will still gladly accept a title of nobility when the opportunity presents itself. Catherine Ashton is a recent example.

decentralization, subsidiarity, colonialism, etc. Apart from some nuances in terminology and some variations in intensity, the politicians of both the left and the right—at least those who today qualify as such—agree on all of these things. The political party that would attack one of these dogmas would be subject to defamation campaigns and ostracized by the dominant parties.

Hence, there is a great misunderstanding which follows from the various qualifiers we assign to different political persuasions. Today we no longer hesitate to call a classical liberal party "conservative" and suggest it is on the right. It is evidently of little concern to many that a good number of "socialist" politicians are also millionaires. We call people we find too conservative "fascists" although fascism is on the left and conservatism is on the right. We qualify populism as "extreme right" even though it does not renounce the welfare state, which is a creation of the left. The lines are all blurred, perhaps by design, but the reality is that the political ideologies the voters fight over do not offer any genuine alternatives.

What aggravates this confusion even further is that the characteristics of the left and the right are often jumbled. We attribute to the right a nationalistic tendency when nationalism is a trait of the left that came about during the French Revolution. Traditionally, the right is not nationalist; rather, it is patriotic. One criticizes the right today for being globalist, and therefore internationalist, when this is one of the characteristics of Marxism. Similarly, it was the left, during the French Revolution, which excessively centralized the government in order to obliterate any trace of regionalism; but under Franco it was the Spanish left that resorted to regionalism in order to oppose the right's centralization (though the Carlists, on the traditional right, had also historically championed regionalism).

Also, since democracy naturally moves leftward and one has a better chance of being elected by making promises and playing on the population's passions and fears rather than calling for reason and sacrifice, all nuances in political persuasions inevitably gravitate to the left in democracy. This is so true that the parties sometimes crowd to the left, thereby leaving the right vacant. One qualifies as right parties which, without being completely socialist, defend all of the advances made by the left and have themselves become champions of the welfare state.

In *Manifesto of the Communist Party*, written in Brussels and published in London in 1848, Karl Marx and Friedrich Engels listed ten steps that should be adopted by governments desiring to put communism into practice. These steps have almost all been adopted by parliamentary democracies in various forms. They cannot be called into question today without causing serious upheaval.

1. Abolition of property in land and application of all rents of land to public purposes.

2. A heavy progressive or graduated income tax.

3. Abolition of all right of inheritance.

4. Confiscation of the property of all emigrants and rebels.

5. Centralisation of credit in the hands of the State, by means of a national bank with State capital and an exclusive monopoly.

6. Centralisation of the means of communication and transport in the hands of the State.

7. Extension of factories and instruments of production owned by the State; the bringing into cultivation of waste lands, and the improvement of the soil generally in accordance with a common plan.

8. Equal liability of all to labour. Establishment of industrial armies, especially for agriculture.

9. Combination of agriculture with manufacturing industries; gradual abolition of the distinction between town and country, by a more equable distribution of the population over the country.

10. Free education for all children in public schools. Abolition of children's factory labour in its present form. Combination of education with industrial production, etc., etc.[6]

Marxism was applied brutally in Eastern Europe. It was imposed by means of a revolution so that the

---

[6] Karl Marx and Frederick Engels, *Manifesto of the Communist Party*, ed. Frederick Engels (Chicago: Charles H. Kerr & Company, 1906), 45-46.

transition from the first state (for most countries, a monarchical and relatively traditional society) to the communist state was done rapidly and induced a considerable mental shock. Until the mid-twentieth century, a large portion of the Russian population still held on to a keepsake that had a specific enough tie to Czarist Russia. They genuinely missed what had been, despite the continuous Marxist propaganda. Memory played all that much more of an important role given the rapidity and brutality of the transition.

In Western Europe, on the other hand, the socialist transformation was accomplished gradually, by means of successive strokes. Great care was taken to introduce the reforms in such a way so that they appeared entirely justified. If one had talked of 50% taxation or legal abortion in 1930, or even in 1950, it would have provoked an almost universal reaction of disgust. The sensibilities of our grandparents would have been revolted by such reforms. Now they are practiced daily and amidst general indifference. A large portion of the population considers these measures completely justified.

But let us go back to the measures prescribed in *Manifesto of the Communist Party.*

1. *Abolition of property in land and application of all rents of land to public purposes.* We have not been subject, in Western Europe, to total expropriation of private property, but it has been divided up or destroyed by successoral laws and succession fees, and gnawed away at through taxation. Private real property is taxed three times: upon acquisition, during

possession, and upon hereditary transfer. It is a slow and systematic expropriation to the benefit of the state.

2. *A heavy progressive or graduated income tax.* The taxing of income, progressively or by bracket, is today widespread in Western Europe.

3. *Abolition of all right of inheritance.* Not abolished but gnawed away at so much that efforts to build up the family fortune must begin anew with each generation.

4. *Confiscation of the property of all emigrants and rebels.* Not applied systematically. Let us only point out that the property of expatriates who fled the communists at the end of the Second World War was generally not ceded back after the fall of communism. Little or no compensation was offered. The Czech Republic, in fact, recently obtained a guarantee from the European Union that it had no obligation to the descendants of the 3.5 million Sudeten Germans who were expelled and had their property confiscated.

5. *Centralisation of credit in the hands of the State, by means of a national bank with State capital and an exclusive monopoly.* Central banks, fiat money, legal tender, and the absence of the gold standard have today become incontestable rules of finance. Commercial banks apply the rules decreed by the state.

6. *Centralisation of the means of communication and transport in the hands of the State.* This has been done. The majority of public transport is either the

property of the state or under its tight control. The same applies to means of mass communication, which is much more important than other services in Marxist thought.

7. *Extension of factories and instruments of production owned by the State; the bringing into cultivation of waste lands, and the improvement of the soil generally in accordance with a common plan.* This measure still by and large has relevance today when one considers the business world's state of dependency with respect to the state, and the immense regulatory powers of the latter.

8. *Equal liability of all to labour. Establishment of industrial armies, especially for agriculture.* Here, the passage of time has had its effects. One cannot blame Marx for not having foreseen the advances in technology. However, this measure still applies very well to our society, where professional work has become a genuine kind of servitude. Society has become considerably proletarianized, so much so that almost everyone is required to work just to make ends meet. In most families, both the man and the woman must work in order to provide for the needs of the household. Is this progress?

9. *Combination of agriculture with manufacturing industries; gradual abolition of the distinction between town and country, by a more equable distribution of the population over the country.* This surprising measure finds an echo in our professional-izing of studies and in the obligation to transform

every field into a money-making venture (education, the arts and humanities, sports, etc.). As for the difference between the city and the country, it has faded indeed, so much so that it has completely disappeared in the most populous regions of Western Europe. Authentic country life, with its rugged spirit of independence, its traditions, its distrust of modernity, and its penchant for self-sufficiency, has completely disappeared, and with it, the most robust opposition to all state centralization, whether it be classical liberal or Marxist. One must not forget that Marx despised country folk as much as the bourgeoisie.

10. *Free education for all children in public schools. Abolition of children's factory labour in its present form. Combination of education with industrial production, etc., etc.* Compulsory free education, a creation of the left, is today a fait accompli in all of Europe. Depending on the individual country, any other form of education (private or homeschooling) is either looked upon with suspicion or forbidden outright. It is remarkable that Marx did not condemn child industrial labor in principle, but only as it was practiced in his time.

This little detour through *Manifesto of the Communist Party* serves to show how with the passing of time classical liberal democracy, as it was conceived in the nineteenth century, has been considerably transformed and assimilated into the grand scheme of Karl Marx's revolutionary program. Today the Western world lives in a mixed system composed of both classical liberalism and Marxism. Some find it too far to the right while others find it too far to the left. Most probably have only a very faint idea of what a true system of freedom and responsibility would look like, such as that desired by classical liberalism, and most also seem to have already forgotten what a communist hell it was without freedom or private property. The fact that the current system is mixed does not mean it is moderate and acceptable. It is quite capable of bringing together the vices of the two constituent systems rather than their virtues.

There is also confusion today between capitalism and classical liberalism. Many people, even in right-wing and populist circles, consider it good form to incriminate capitalism. Capitalism, however, is an excellent thing. It proceeds from respect for private property. As capitalism is the reinvestment of saved money for the purpose of making new profits, it presupposes respect for property rights and free enterprise. It has existed in Europe since the Middle Ages and has contributed significantly to the development of Western society. One would have a hard time, moreover, finding someone who is not a capitalist, that is to say someone who has no instinct for property and only an aversion to profit.

But what one ought to designate as bad capitalism is the concentration of wealth and the power this wealth procures. This danger does not stem from capitalism itself but rather from parliamentary democracy, for it is democracy that enables money powers to dominate the political realm. This inherent defect did not exist at the time of traditional monarchy, and it was precisely for this reason that traditional monarchy was overthrown.

In other words, capitalism only becomes harmful when it grants political power to the money powers. This was only made possible thanks to the advent of parliamentary democracy, which was an invention of liberalism. It is therefore the foundational principles of political liberalism (equality before the law, suppression of privileges, centralization of political power, censitary suffrage, and the accountability of ministers to the legislative houses) which have enabled the rise of a wealthy class and its power over society.

Classical liberalism—like socialism—is an ideology, that is to say a system of thought held to be true and beneficial for man *a priori*, without having to be proven as such. An ideology rests on principles that are generally false or poorly conceived. With respect to classical liberalism, the false principle is the primacy of liberty, viewed as an end in itself rather than as a means. Classical liberalism also claims that the pursuit of individual profit contributes to the service of the common good just as much as an organic society under the authority of an independent arbiter. With respect to the ideology of socialism, its primacy of equality is both unjust and contrary to nature. These two systems were imposed on Western societies through revolutionary means with the professed goal of making man happier, and this even against his will, by transforming society and, if possible, man himself.

Classical liberalism, however, is not incompatible with a socialist system or a mixed system like the welfare state. Socialism did not come to mitigate the excesses of classical liberalism; it came only to displace them. The two systems are easily superimposed over each other. As socialism is nothing other than state capitalism, the mixed system that is the welfare state feels all of the effects of interventionism, taxation, and legislative abuse which put the population in a state of dependence vis-à-vis the state. In 1900, Europe by and large lived under a classical liberal and capitalist system. There were large capitalists but also a multitude of too often forgotten small capitalists. They could, thanks to their professional income, put money aside, become owners, and end up living off of income derived from their capital. It must be noted that this middle class has today become proletarian to the extent that it cannot live without assistance from the state, which assumes the role of super-boss. In 1900, a portion of society was certainly made up of system losers, the proletariat who depended on their bosses. They represented a minority of the population, certainly not negligible. Aside from this minority, there was the rest of society, which showcased capitalism in all of its varying degrees. Today, the composition of society is inverted: the majority is a middle class that has in reality become proletarian with respect to the state; at the same time there remains a minority of very rich people who evade the grip of the social state through the power wealth provides and through legal artifices their international position affords them.

Therefore, the socialization of society has not caused the power of wealth proper to the classical liberal system to disappear. It has only proletarianized the middle class. Classical liberalism and socialism operate on different levels. The bulk of the population, a middle class living in dependence on the state, is subject to a socialist system, while a financial elite—the only true capitalists of today—are able to free themselves from this system, or even to dictate the system's rules thanks to their financial influence.

The danger, then, of concentrating wealth in the hands of a small number of individuals or corporations which become richer or more powerful than the state still remains in a welfare state. It is a common reality and very much adaptable to a mixed system. Today the money powers no longer hold power by means of censitary suffrage, but rather by means of the pressure they continuously exert on politicians through lobbying and corruption. All of this has become possible only because of parliamentary democracy.

Parliamentary democracy was the system par excellence of classical liberalism. It was instituted to serve the interests of the capitalist bourgeoisie—censitary suffrage, the prohibition against all forms of corporatism, and the stranglehold of money on politics all testify to this fact.

To believe Marxism would be capable of correcting this tendency is pure fantasy, for in Marxism are found the same relativism and the same materialism; there is also the same absence of fixed values promoted and defended by an arbiter of the common good. It should not be surprising then that these two ideologies of Marxism and classical liberalism have found space for common life within parliamentary democracy. Since this is an accomplished fact, it can be said that parliamentary democracy has found its point of convergence, the meeting of left and right, in a soft totalitarianism—soft at least for the moment—which has reduced the majority of the population to a new form of slavery, in order to give the money powers and their political lackeys the greatest advantage. This is the end of democracy.

Chapter 7

"DECIVILIZATION"

DEMOCRACY is a system that bases its decisions on the number of votes, on quantity rather than quality. It is a system that has no fundamental understanding of the concept of goodness. Instead of posing the questions: "Is this decision good? Is this opinion just?" it asks rather: "How many favor this decision or this opinion?" Democracy, in its decision-making process, does not seek the good but numbers. Or rather, being unable to define the good, it surrenders its discovery to numbers, so that the good in democracy becomes what pleases the greatest number. This fundamental relativism is the basis of democracy. It fits into a belief system where the very notions of truth and goodness are inconsistent. At best, democracy can only *temporarily* obtain peace in society by imposing the majority opinion on the submitting minority. At no moment can it claim that it is seeking, discovering, and imposing the good.

One might object that democracy, in its decision-making process, puts its trust in each voter's or each representative's sense of the good. This is to forget, however, that private interest is the deciding factor. In democracy, the voter seeks to satisfy his own private interests rather than to do what is best for the common good. Each voter votes according to what he expects from the state. The representative either does the same or takes orders from his party or groups of influence, which pursue their own particular interests as well. And the totality of these particular interests does not amount to the common good, but to an unmanageable mass of contradictions.

It is remarkable to consider that democracy is a uniquely political phenomenon. It is only in politics that decisions are made by means of universal suffrage. In every other human community, be it family, school, business, the civil service, or the military, decisions are never made this way. We rely on authority that is derived from age, responsibility, fittingness, or competence, but never on an authority that is derived from numbers. This does not preclude consultation prior to making a decision, but it is not numbers that ultimately have the most weight. Has anyone ever heard of a business where the major decisions are made by giving the cleaning ladies and doormen the same vote as the managers and directors? Has anyone ever heard of a family or a school that left its major decisions up to the vote of the majority—the children? This is, however, how democracy claims to operate.

Everywhere, except in politics, decisions are made on the basis of competence, seniority, fittingness, or on any other rational criteria that would give one reason to believe the best possible decision will be made. In politics, however, it is simply assumed that any elected official, regardless of his qualifications or reasons for acting, is capable of making decisions which will best serve the common good. There are, moreover, no specific qualifications required to be elected. Paradoxically, the very individuals on whom the fate of millions of citizens depends can be the least qualified and most ignorant people in the world.

Here we touch on one of the absurdities of the democratic system. All of Western civilization was built on the principle of competence, in other words on the differentiation and complementarity of educational backgrounds, experiences, and personalities. But democracy does not take this principle into consideration, for it indifferently gives the right to vote to the eighteen-year-old high schooler as to the retiree, to the businessman as to the unemployed person, to the homeowner as to the renter, and even today to the citizen as to the foreigner. Any consideration of the voter's ability to discern the common good, and therefore to define the very object of politics, is simply put to the side. Quite logically, the elected official also benefits from this same principle of non-competence by the fact that he is not required to demonstrate any particular skills relating to governance or to the development of legislation. It is assumed he is competent in every domain, which explains, for example, why the same minister can go from one ministry to another performing equally poorly and without having the least bit of competence appropriate for the positions.

But it is not just a matter of competence. If there are such things as good and bad political decisions, we would want to entrust power to those best able to discern what the common good is and to make decisions which serve it. Thus, we would seek to confide power to people who are upright, impartial, qualified, and, most importantly, of such excellent moral character that we have reason to expect the best possible decisions from them. Democracy, however, follows yet again a completely different path, and we are forced to acknowledge that the aforementioned qualities are not traits for which political personnel and democratic leaders are particularly well known.

This is not by accident. In the functioning of democracy, there is this paradox: the qualities necessary to ascend to power through democratic vote are precisely what make for defective leaders. To rise to the head of a political party and to win elections at the national level, one must pander to the voters and tell them not what is, but what they want to hear. One must bow down to particular interests, especially to those of the money powers. One must not let any scruples get in the way; one must be about superficial externals rather than about substance; one must also be devoted to one's party. It is not necessary to have acquired any skills for governing; it is even better not to have them, for that might be indicative of professional integrity. These characteristics of the successful democratic candidate, however, are precisely the defects one does not want to see in a statesman. The good statesman, by way of contrast, must be realistic, honest, incorruptible, conscientious, a person who is about substance rather than superficial externals, and someone not too easily influenced; he must especially be impartial so as to serve the common good. It is essential that he has acquired the skills for governing. This is why the men and women democracy puts in power tend to be precisely those a sane system would keep far from it.

For this reason, not only is democracy incapable of choosing the most suitable persons for governing, but it even tends to select the worst and to reject the worthy. It thus functions as a backwards filter that raises the bad to the highest government offices while keeping the good at the lowest echelons of the party or even outside its ranks.

This break in the rational control of authority is troubling. It makes one think political power was intentionally entrusted to malleable and versatile individuals who would be incapable of exercising their own judgment and taking a firm stand, and who would be ever ready to negotiate everything, so that they would be the last people in the world capable of resisting pressure from particular interests. In fact, if one had wanted to have representatives and political leaders who could be conveniently used by all kinds of interests foreign to the common good, one would have simply invented parliamentary democracy.

Democracy appears then as an anomaly in human behavior. It is cut off from the natural order insofar as man very rarely resorts to it outside of politics and almost always prefers another mode of decision-making. One naturally has recourse to voting only in extreme cases where it is impossible to discover the good, or where the good does not exist but only opinion. Voting must be practiced on a small scale, in confined human communities and organizations. The more a community grows though in importance and organizational complexity, the less one ought to resort to voting, for competence then becomes a crucial element of decision-making. The state, however, which is the most complex and most extensive of human communities, does in fact resort to voting and does not require its deciders to have any particular competence.

This is not natural, for it is unreasonable, and the use of reason is consonant with human nature. It is contrary, or at the very least offensive, to human reason to surrender decisions important for everyone to electoral chance. To renounce reason in such decisions, which is also to renounce serious reflection, experience, and competence, is folly, if not criminal.

Civilization is the product of the continuous labor of man's will and reason in the pursuit of the good. It is self-evident that each individual pursues the good proper to himself, such as the good of his family or success in his profession. Every business seeks profit and prosperity. Every human initiative seeks success and the attainment of the goal for which it was formed. This is true for individual persons as well as for associations and organizations, both big and small. Some organizations, such as churches and charitable groups, seek the good of others all while serving their own good, which is to fulfill the mission in which they are invested.

If all of these efforts aimed at the good arise freely, societies will give themselves a form of government which supports their efforts, or at the very least does not obstruct them. They will want a government that itself also seeks the good and is capable of doing so. It will thus be a government founded on the same principles which govern society—principles such as competence, responsibility, and ownership. This government will have the means to discern the common good and will have the necessary independence to serve it.

If the private good is sought out naturally and zealously by individuals and all emanations of their free activity (families, local communities, businesses, professional associations, charitable organizations, schools, universities, etc.), with each level of association seeking to serve its own good, the only good that is not yet pursued is the common good. It is the role of the sovereign authority to serve the common good, meaning that which is in the interest of all, common to all, above all, without necessarily being the composite of all private goods, which would be an absurd and impossible operation.

The common good is precisely that without which civilization cannot come into being, for it is indispensable to all private initiatives. Without the common good ensured, the private initiatives of man cannot develop freely, for he is in fear of losing the fruits of his labor. The first condition necessary for a civilization's development is that man is able to have confidence in the next day.

Note that the state, whose order in time corresponds to its place in the hierarchy of values, comes *after* the natural and traditional institutions of the family, the village, the business, and every other community and association man is capable of freely creating and developing. The state is not the author, much less the owner, of these institutions; it is their servant. It comes to fill the void left when all the natural interests and needs of man are already served and taken charge of by his free initiative. The state comes to bring the final service of peace so that society can freely advance in material prosperity, in knowledge and the arts, and in its spiritual vocation.

The state's true place is defined by the principle of subsidiarity. The state renders a service that society cannot or does not want to render, either because it is not its role or because it has better things to do. And this role of the state is to keep the peace.

One might be surprised that this single term of "peace" can sum up all the functions of the state, but, in reality, it is a considerable role. The state must maintain peace first of all vis-à-vis other states by means of diplomacy and military might. Then it must maintain peace inside its borders by enforcing laws through a judicial system and a police force—it is thus in charge of public security and order. It must likewise defend the integrity of private property, which is a foundation of freedom and prosperity. The state must also ensure social peace by maintaining the established natural order without seeking to overthrow it. Finally, the state must also provide certain public services (communications, postal service, etc.) which, if they were to be privately monopolized, would risk holding the population hostage and endangering public peace. The role of the state stops right about here.

A civilization, in other words, can only develop when there is peace. If it were necessary to define in a single word the common good, which is the supreme responsibility of the sovereign authority and the state, that word would be "peace." Based on this single responsibility of the state, one can easily define its prerogatives and delimit its sphere of activity.

The democratic state cannot serve the common good or guarantee peace, for in order to do so it would have to act independently, competently, and benevolently, which it is incapable of doing. To serve the common good, it needs to have at the minimum an impartial arbiter, and this office is non-existent in parliamentary democracy. And without an impartial arbiter who is competent, responsible, and has a sufficient degree of independence, serving the common good is impossible.

Furthermore, the democratic state bears within itself an appetite for unlimited power, induced by electioneering and justified by the principle of popular rule. It is marked by a kind of legislative and administrative bulimia; there is nothing to curb it in its roles of assisting and regulating. Nothing escapes its specter, for it claims to embody the will of the people. It is driven by the reckless pursuit of votes in its favor, and, in this race for power, it divides society into rival factions and ideologies.

Hence, the democratic state does exactly the opposite of what is necessary for serving the common good. On the one hand, it succumbs to the most powerful private interests, and, on the other hand, it engulfs and infects all of society, depriving it of the liberty necessary to further its particular interests.

It is insane, therefore, to grant such an expansive power to a state which cannot pursue the good on account of its relativism and which, by its very manner of operating, drifts inevitably towards totalitarianism. If one adds to this the fact that the democratic state is in reality only a smokescreen behind which powers act to exploit the democratic system for their own particular ends, it becomes undeniable that democracy is the most deceptive and dangerous political system ever invented.

At the beginning of the twentieth century, democracy was not yet a significantly widespread phenomenon. Most European nations were under a monarchy and universal suffrage was still very uncommon. Democracy presented itself as a limited phenomenon in the political sphere, an anomaly of sorts whose history was only beginning. Society as a whole still exhibited a strong attachment to traditional values as they pertained to family, business, and morality in general. But following the First World War, the democratic virus gradually spread from the political sphere to society as a whole. The first totalitarian states appeared. The democratization of governments only strengthened money powers and ideologies. Events following the Second World War were also marked by the spirit of revolution, which was encouraged considerably by the fact that the Soviet Union had been on the winning side. And so the process of degradation in Western societies, European society especially, did not cease to gather momentum until it resulted in the state of decadence we know today.

What has the democratic state made of this society over which it has extended its empire? Has it sought to preserve it from moral degradation, or from the onslaughts of ideologies and particular interests? Has it established safeguards to protect the populations from the consumerism, indebtedness, and inflation which have served the money powers? The democratic state has done none of these things. On the contrary, it has become the docile servant of these forces and has put its political and legislative powers at their service. The democratic state, having no arbiter and having completely whored itself over to the interests of parties and pressure groups, is probably the form of government which, in the course of history, has most betrayed the populations entrusted to it. It is also the one which has contributed most to their decadence.

The democratic state has patiently but relentlessly worked to undermine the traditional structure of European society. Wherever it has extended its empire, it has infringed on individual liberty and responsibility, private property, and free enterprise. Its grip on opinion, education, and culture has led to irreparable damage. The democratic state has everywhere imposed egalitarianism, moral relativism, legal conformity, the debasement of culture, and the reduction of individual freedoms, all for its own profit.

The degradation in the arts and humanities has been brought about by the vulgarization of taste, which is itself the direct result of social egalitarianism and the dumbing down of education to the lowest common denominator. The public funding of art aggravates this decadent trend since state initiatives have to appeal to the masses. Government management of culture has resulted in the disaster we are witnessing today: the degradation of language, the vanishing of the humanist spirit, the dearth of good authors, the decadence in music and the fine arts, the disappearance of poetry, and so forth.

Free and compulsory public education, that is to say education subsidized and regulated by the state, is largely responsible for all of this. Unable to lay claim to a principle of excellence (which would be unacceptably elitist) and not having the freedom necessary to differentiate, education is marked by a dumbing down and a sterilizing conformism. The freedom of schools to choose curricula, teaching methods, textbooks, disciplinary styles, schedules, teachers, and so forth is almost non-existent, and it results in an absence of competition and innovation. Everyone must conform to preconceived models and ideas coming from the heads of politically appointed officials. As a result, the caliber of instruction has declined considerably with each passing generation, and it continues to do so.[1] Today many students admitted into universities lack basic knowledge and skills in reading, writing, mathematics and science; their ignorance on matters of general culture, which is an issue unto itself, is ever worsening. Politically correct ideological principles are given priority over objective knowledge and skills. The state makes use of schools to fashion conforming voters, malleable consumers, and docile taxpayers, not free and educated citizens.

Do these words seem exaggerated? Or to put the question differently, is it to be doubted that democracy has had a role in the decline of education? This very phenomenon, however, was also perceived by Alexis de Tocqueville when he wrote:

> The state receives, and often takes, the child from the arms of the mother to hand it over to official agents; the state undertakes to train the heart and to instruct the mind of each generation. Uniformity prevails in the

---

[1] See the Organization for Economic Cooperation and Development's Program for International Student Assessment surveys, which shed light on the inexorable decline in the quality of education in most so-called developed countries.

courses of public instruction as in everything else; diversity as well as freedom is disappearing day by day.[2]

The family is the foundation upon which all of civilization is built. It is the primordial place of human development. Nothing useful to man happens without it, much less acts against it. The process of social dissolution in which the democratic state is engaged, after having almost annihilated society's traditional structures, has ended in attacking this foundation which is the family.

The family was first reduced to its most basic unit of just parents and children, very far removed from the institution still known in the eighteenth and nineteenth centuries, which was not just a nuclear family but also family in the larger sense to include multiple generations with lateral branches, and even domestic servants.

Divorce, free unions, contraception, and the general revolution in morals are already old developments. Phenomena such as stepfamilies, commonly practiced cohabitation, abortion, homosexual unions (with the legal right to adopt children), and surrogate mothers are present-day realities which the democratic state does nothing to oppose, although these things are detrimental to children (being linked to problems such as emotional frailty, individualism,

---

[2] Alexis de Tocqueville, "That Among the European Nations of Our Time the Sovereign Power Is Increasing, Although the Sovereigns Are Less Stable," vol. II, bk. 4, chap. V in *Democracy in America*. Translated by Henry Reeve. (New York: Colonial Press, 1899), xroads.virginia.edu/~HYPER/DETOC/ch4_05.htm.

skepticism, academic failure, alcoholism, and suicide) and bring down the birthrate considerably.

Democratic egalitarianism has produced feminism and the so-called liberation of the woman through financial independence and careerism. Family incomes are eroding due to inflation and the heavy taxation levied by the welfare state, forcing both parents into the workplace. A family's patrimony is eaten away at with each passing generation. Little space remains for children, who according to the consumerist mindset are burdensome and an obstacle to the enjoyment of life.

With the family so weakened, the state steps in as a substitute. Small children are taken care of by the state in day care centers and nursery schools, as are the elderly in nursing homes. In times past, these services were provided by the family. The pension of retired persons is guaranteed by the state, as are unemployment benefits for those without work. Both school and television, which are the principal channels of instruction for children and adolescents, are under state control. The family, as a place for the transmission of values, memories, patrimony, and good morals, has largely been subjugated by the omnipresent state. Since the state now covers risks and provides services which were previously assumed exclusively by the family, the latter, regarded as useless, has withdrawn to a minimal role of providing housing, food, leisure, and parental affection. The traditional values of responsibility, foresight, morals, work, solidarity, patrimony, and honor are discouraged by the fact that the state has taken charge and rendered all efforts on the part of the family ineffectual. The democratic state, in effect, assumes responsibility and foresight instead of the people; it dictates its morality to them; it helps them to find a job and supports them when they lose one; it ensures solidarity through state agencies and expropriates a considerable portion of private patrimony.

The dissolution of the family is a work spearheaded by the democratic state. The proper role of the state is not to espouse individualistic tendencies or to satisfy the demands of influential minorities. Its role is to defend the most vulnerable (such as children) and to safeguard the general interest for the long-term. It does this, for example, by ensuring the birthrate is sufficiently high for generational replacement. Its role is to defend the institution of the family, which is indispensable to the health of the entire social body. An arbiter of the common good would have ensured this, but the democratic state has allied itself with destructive forces acting against the general interest.

The declining birthrate, which inevitably accompanies the erosion of the family institution, is perhaps the most consequential damage since it could lead to society's disappearance through extinction. When the demographic collapse of Western countries appeared inevitable, the money powers began pressuring governments to encourage immigration. In reality, the allurement of the demographic void coupled with the welfare state's lavish handouts was already more than sufficient to get immigration under way, and on an unprecedented scale. Governments, however, could have blocked this through restrictive immigration legislation in conjunction with resolute domestic policies favoring higher birthrates. They have done exactly the opposite: they have tightened their chokehold on native families and have invited foreigners to come in and replace them.

The non-representative character of democracy is particularly well illustrated by the phenomenon of immigration. As with other major decisions of democratic states, the fact that immigrant populations are admitted in or invited arises from a particularly limited and biased view of the common good. A goal of immigration is in effect to procure cheap labor and keep down wages for low-skilled jobs. Yet another goal is to maintain, and even increase, the sales of basic consumer goods, something which the European population growth rates no longer guarantee. Immigration also serves to keep up real estate prices, which would otherwise tend to fall for the same reasons. Moreover, immigration greatly contributes to the disappearance of national identity and the breaking up of the social body, which can only benefit the state in the short-term. By considering the sectors of the economy affected by immigration, it is easy to identify the people who benefit most from it. They are the very same people behind the immigration policies. The democratic state does, of course, see a relatively short-lived ideological advantage in this; however, to the detriment of the taxpayer, it must bear resulting additional costs pertaining to unemployment, housing, integration, and public safety and security.

Immigration is indicative of a kind of criminal irresponsibility typical in democracy. At no moment have the native populations been consulted about immigration, which has been an unpopular phenom-enon from the beginning. This is proof of the democratic state's ability to impose a state of affairs on the people which they would have spontaneously rejected had they been consulted. By means of media propaganda, it is possible for the democratic state to at least obtain the majority of the population's acquiescence, if not their outright approval.

The only immigration that ought to be considered acceptable is that done by invitation. Rather than the state imposing on the native population the presence and the costs of an immigrant population it does not want, it ought to be the native population itself, via businesses, that invites the immigrants and assumes responsibility for them, acting as their guarantor. If things were to happen this way, immigrant labor would only be facilitated in cases of genuine need, and the assimilation of these foreigners into society would occur quickly and without mishap. But once again, those who have made our current pro-immigration policies are not the ones now bearing the burden. Today they enjoy the luxurious and carefree retirement of ministers and presidents, and no one holds them accountable for their totally irresponsible and immeasurably consequential decisions.

Immigration is certainly not the only phenomenon capable of plunging European civilization into chaos. Other catastrophes generated by democracy may occur, such as a grave economic crisis, hyperinflation, or a shortage of energy resources. These would only aggravate and accelerate the process of dissolution, already well under way, of a society considerably weakened spiritually, morally, intellectually, and materially. A combination of these various causes and the chaos that would inevitably ensue could therefore be fatal for European civilization.

In such a situation, the democratic state, with its bureaucracy, its exorbitant costs, and its political elite who will have made their escape, will be of no assistance to a population that is as helpless as it is accustomed to depending on the state for all of its needs. These scourges, then, could befall a particularly vulnerable population which has forgotten all instincts of solidarity and survival.

This might just become democracy's ultimate accomplishment in Europe: the death and disappearance of civilization on the continent.

Chapter 8

FUTURE PROSPECTS

SOME might ask: Why do political leaders not see that this downward spiral will result in the total destruction of society and, ultimately, in the destruction of democracy itself?

To ask this question is to credit our elected leaders with the loftiness of vision and high moral standards the majority of them do not have. It is to identify oneself with our elected leaders, which is a rather naive thing to do. If the voter only knew what kind of individuals his elected officials truly were, he would likely be horrified at the great chasm which separates them from him.

Parliamentary democracy rarely produces true statesmen, as its party system more often promotes ambitious and self-interested persons, demagogues, and even communication experts. These are generally superficial and egocentric individuals with a very limited understanding of society and man. These politicians do not have the makings of statesmen. They are adventurers who use the state to satiate their hunger for power and money or to benefit their party. It may happen by chance that democracy allows an idealistic, upright, and competent individual to come to power, someone like the former Colombian president Alvaro Uribe or the former Polish president

Lech Kaczynski[1]—rare and fleeting personalities hardly appreciated at the international level precisely because they do not lend themselves to all of the political game-playing.

Does democracy have the power in and of itself to reverse its march towards its own demise? This is what many hope for, either because they excessively trust in the quality of this political ideology or because they fear having to consider options other than democracy.

Democracy has the natural ability to kill itself. It behaved thus in post-revolutionary France and Russia, and in a completely legal manner in Germany in the 1930s. But might it also favor a return to reality and the cession of power to true servants of the common good?

In Europe, the only political forces today which could, in the most extreme of circumstances, assume this rescue role are found on the side of populism. Conservative in its values, sometimes classically liberal when it is a matter of opposing the stifling interventionism of the state, and yet ready to defend social gains (which wins it the appreciation of workers and the middle classes), populism is the only political current which comes to the defense of those interests of the population denied or ignored by the parties in power.

Populist parties, from the simple fact that they can bring together voters from both the left and the right, have a chance of coming to power in the near enough future. The deterioration of security conditions in

---

[1] There are some promising leaders currently in power who also come to mind. Since time will ultimately tell if they meet expectations, we will refrain from mentioning them by name.

Europe due to mass immigration plays in their favor. But the European political establishment is extremely wary of these parties and less and less secretly acknowledges that they represent a danger to the continuity of the ruling political class.

When it feels itself threatened in this way, democracy has recourse to three stratagems which have been sufficiently effective thus far. The first consists in not allowing the threatening party to express itself. It is deprived of access to the media, and new electoral laws are enacted to thwart it (such as requiring at least five percent of the vote to have proportional parliamentary representation, a requirement to collect signatures, the denial of public subsidies, and the outlawing of certain kinds of political rhetoric). When this first stratagem does not work and the party manages to get members into elected office, there is then recourse to a systematic smear campaign based on lies and calumnies, that is to say the demonization of the party, which will be accused of racism, fascism, and other modern-day capital sins.[2] If this second stratagem does not

---

[2] Recall Belgium's Louis Michel declaring that Jörg Haider's Freedom Party of Austria did not have the right to participate in its own country's government even though the party obtained 26.9% of the vote in Austria and 41.2% in the state of Carinthia—while Louis Michel's own party only had 10.1% of the vote in Belgium. The French have witnessed for years how supposedly democratic parties completely block their competition and deprive them of access to power. In certain countries like Germany and Austria, certain kinds of statements are punishable by law, which literally deprives some parties of their freedom of speech. In the Netherlands, the populist leader Geert Wilders was hauled off to court for having brought to light the Koran's incitement of murder and hatred. In Belgium, parties not belonging to the club in power

adequately do the job—though this is generally as far as things need to go, since the democratic state has at its disposal a media arsenal capable of destroying any chances of a threatening party among the voters— there is still the option of assassination. The deaths of populist leaders such as Pim Fortuyn and Jörg Haider[3] suggest that democracy today no longer recoils from murder when all other deterrents have failed. The democratic state's control of the media and police force always allows assassinations to pass as mere accidents or as acts of the mentally ill.

For the European populist parties currently gaining influence, it is likely that these measures will be ineffective. Thus, we could witness a political earth-quake in the near future if one or another of these parties ascends to power.

Populism represents a danger for the political class in place because it threatens not only their power but also the particular interests of their bosses. Populism does not show itself ready to compromise the national interest, and therefore reveals itself better able to serve the common good than the private interests of pressure groups. But the reason the democratic political class exists is precisely to be ever ready to renounce the national interest in favor of particular interests, primarily those of the internationalists and the globalists.

There is no way of knowing if the European populists' disinterestedness and unwillingness to compromise will last. If the system's stratagems do not

---

are denounced as "undemocratic" and a *cordon sanitaire* is implemented to try to contain them.

[3] See chap. 5, n. 10.

work or are not fully utilized, one must still not neglect its power of seduction. Power, in a democracy, is an ideal path towards personal enrichment, and the populists are as susceptible as anyone else to the allurement of money. It is thus to be feared that the populists, although so ardent in their defense of national identity and national interests today, might one day themselves be corrupted by power when they have access to it. They would then resemble those Marxists or environmentalists who, by investing themselves in the democratic state, have become its devoted servants. They certainly had an influence on society, but they never produced the sweeping changes they heralded.

Populism, regardless of the successes it promises, cannot, however, be expected to fix the root of the problem and to replace democracy with a system based on nature and reason. It does not promise to put an end to the absurdity of the electoral system, nor to the escape from political accountability, nor to the absence of an arbiter. There is little chance, then, it will do anything effective against the oligarchy and, consequently, against the inevitable submission of the democratic state to the money powers. Or, if it tries to do so, one can imagine the money powers will use all means at their disposal to defend their interests. Despite this, populism can at least act as a step towards the abolition of parliamentary democracy and the establishment of a system that is more mindful of reality.

Are there other forces out there capable of bringing about a return to the service of the common good?

Christian democracy's vision of a democracy subject to moral principles which would limit its powers and safeguard both its morals and its liberty is a pipe dream. No limits on the democratic state's powers do or can exist, except those it freely chooses to impose on itself. Any limits beyond these would contradict the principle of popular sovereignty.

Some think Christianity has a vocation to imbue democracy with values. They are right in theory, but they will labor in vain, for democracy is a relativistic system and is hostile to any moral constraints it has not given itself.

What is more, Christians do not today constitute a real threat to democracy; on the contrary, they are its victims, something they are not yet ready to acknowledge. Christians working to stop abortion and euthanasia are still far from realizing that if there were a true representation of the people and a truly accountable and impartial executive authority, it is unlikely their fight would have ever been necessary. It is the triumph of some private interests, effectively served by democracy, which has permitted these spectacular advances in immorality. A true arbiter of the common good would have defended the rights of unborn children, and true representation by the people would have shown the disgust of the vast majority for this kind of murder.

John Paul II recalled from time to time that a democracy without values differed little from tyranny,[4] and Benedict XVI denounced the dangers of relativism multiple times. These pontiffs rightly

---

[4] John Paul II, *Evangelium Vitae*, sec. 70.

pointed out that democracy should not be an ideology, but rather a simple system of governance and representation subject to moral imperatives; they made the mistake of believing, however, that democracy was such a system and that it could submit itself to "non-negotiable" values.

Furthermore, since the Second Vatican Council, Rome has opened itself up to the democratic ideology by adopting its notions of human rights, religious liberty, and collegiality, and also by allowing itself to become infected by egalitarianism and secularism. It has considerably weakened itself by doing so. It deprives European civilization of a pole of resistance that could be decisive for its rescue.

The popes generally refer back to a time when democracy was applied to an almost unanimously Christian society and when traditional values gave society its structures and its stability. At the same time, they seem to take no account in their analyses that it was democracy that made way for movements and ideas which have destroyed Christian society. At the end of the nineteenth century, France was an almost 100% Catholic country, yet its radical democratically elected government persecuted the Church. Communism and fascism were implanted in Christian countries thanks to democracy. Revolutionary governments were put in place against the wishes of the majority of populations. Examples demonstrating that democracy favors the best organized minority rather than the majority are so numerous in the history of the last two centuries that one wonders how it is still possible to champion democracy as a representative system.

Moreover, the European population has been very largely dechristianized. It is therefore vain, at this present hour, to hope for a return to the Christian order by means of the democratic process. Democracy, in all of its developments, has shown itself to be much more of an enemy to Christianity than an ally. Nevertheless, we must not underestimate the underlying Christian roots of the people's morals, social life, and common sense. If these roots are incapable today of putting democracy in check, politicians know they must still deal with them carefully. It is also not improbable that the Catholic Church would suddenly come out of her present anemic state and regain her strength, thereby becoming a formidable threat to the democratic ideology. Christians, because of their realism and their moral values, remain, despite everything, the best prepared to serve the common good.

Other forces capable of successfully opposing the democratic system and its deviations do not currently exist in Europe. But democracy is continuously making new enemies for itself. Since the system lies about its true nature and systematically betrays the common good of the populations it administers, it is incompetence, unaccountability, and the excesses of democratic politicians that will stir people up the most against democracy. It is uncertain, however, whether this healthy reaction will be sufficient or come soon enough.

International pressure could also be a decisive factor in the inevitable transformation of the democratic system. But it would accelerate its evolution into a transnational totalitarian state (an evolution that has already been occurring up to this point) rather than encourage its return to a system of national interest. Western democratic governments, especially European governments and the European Union, are now recognizing they have a handicap with respect to countries such as China and Saudi Arabia. These latter countries are also no longer denounced for ideological reasons, such as their disregard for human rights, which proves the West is in a weak position with respect to them. Western governments show themselves to be less efficient on the industrial and commercial levels than their partners on the world stage, for they are incapable of ensuring continuity and following through on policy in the long term. It is political alternation and the breaking up of political power into terms of office that weakens them.

In order to remain on the same level as their competitors, democratic states will have to accelerate their natural evolution towards oligarchy and totalitarianism so that we end up facing three principal types of political systems dominating the world of the twenty-first century: Western style democracy (in its evolved form as a totalitarian state), communism, and Islam.

The communist state as it exists in China and Vietnam is no longer Marxist in the original sense of the term, as it has opened itself up to the free market in order to survive. On the political level, however, it maintains its communist power structure: a single-party system, the absence of free elections, control of the media, and a heavy-handed police state. Some people assure us economic liberalism will put an end to this system. They should not cry victory too quickly. China has become a major partner, whose totalitarian nature all Western countries ceased to denounce from the moment they saw it as a source of profit. Its government is strong and organized. It practices imperialism. It has a political continuity which ensures the long-term survival of the Communist Party's power. The populations of communist states open to the free market are dynamic and not softened by material comfort, social gains, and psychological complexes as are Western populations. They are also younger.[5] Seen from this vantage point, so-called communist governments still have a future.

Furthermore, the decline of the Western world is going to progressively render democracy more uncertain. Democracy is going to lose the ideological aura the Western world had communicated to it back when it was still able to do so.

In the second half of the twentieth century, the democratic ideology was presented to the entire world as the only acceptable option. Every other system was demonized. But the United States and Europe are less and less capable of engaging in this kind of discourse. Their partners include emerging states which have no complex about not being democratic. Thus, this purely Western ideology will be rejected as an exogenous attribute by countries having a non-Western culture, an attribute which they had been required to accept but which they never truly made their own. In these countries, one can expect the emergence of tyrannical governments based on clans, families, parties,

---

[5] The dramatic consequences of China's one-child policy cannot be neglected, however. This policy will soon bring about an economically untenable demographic imbalance.

religious groups, or any other form of oligarchy, and for democratic rituals to be abandoned little by little.

The second type of non-democratic political system which the West can expect is the Islamic regime. Muslim populations are going to be more and more inclined towards a system which is more authentically Islamic, and sharia law will again be established in Muslim states. The political system which will come from this will be completely the opposite of democracy as it survives in the Western imagination. It will be a system whose principles are derived from religion and whose formulation can be found in the Koran and the hadiths. The mixing of the civil and the religious that is proper to Islam will be complete, and Islamic judges will have enormous power. The restoration of the caliphate sounds like a ridiculous pipe dream for many Westerners since it seems so far removed from our modern conception of politics. But this prospect is not so improbable for many Muslims, who see it as the fulfillment of the Islamic political order and are hardly concerned about what Westerners might think.

This Muslim society will have the strength of a religious and ideological consistency which has been lacking for a long time in Western society. It will also have the aggressiveness that comes from religious fanaticism. It will be a formidable enemy for the Western world, and a merciless master. As such, it will even seduce numerous Westerners at a time when parliamentary democracy will reveal its inability to serve the good of peoples.

Confronted with these monolithic systems, the Western world will seek—and it has already started doing so—to replace parliamentary democracy, in such a way that it is still preached but no longer practiced, with a pseudo-democratic totalitarian system. This state will be strong, centralized, interventionist, and a welfare state; it will have stripped the population of its liberties and its purchasing power in exchange for security against the uncertainties of life, as well as from other evils brought about by this state itself. Certainly, democratic externals will be preserved, as will the illusions of liberty and participation in power. After all, the Roman Empire did still keep its senate, did it not?

The European Union is an attempt at this type of state. Even if it were to fail as such, it prefigures the great transnational conglomerates which are destined to administer the Western world in the face of other giant Asian entities.

If democracy in Europe does not disappear by means of an invasion, it will slide slowly into a system of totalitarian oligarchy, which is its natural end result. The democratic myth will only be perpetuated insofar as it makes this transition come about more smoothly. It is an evolution that is inevitable unless a major global upheaval occurs in the meantime or peoples suddenly rise up to thwart the designs of the oligarchs.

In these regimes, especially in the Western regimes, which do not have a communist or Islamic ideology from which they can draw inspiration, corruption will be the chief determining factor of policy. Power will be severed from the peoples and answer to interests which are foreign to them. In these systems that have no national basis, and therefore no real political communities, it is the money powers which will govern through surrogate politicians after having minimized or altogether eliminated the risks tied to elections. The only possible counterbalance might be supplied by ideology or religion. But wherever one or the other is lacking, it will be the hunger for power and money that triumphs.

Regardless, democracy as we have dreamed of it is henceforth a system of the past. It is dead. Gone is this democracy with parliaments genuinely representing the populations, with governments genuinely serving the good of peoples, with a true separation of powers, under the rule of law and with equality for all before the law, with an independent auditing authority and an independent judicial system, with press and education free from government controls, and with a strong civil society that is master of its own destiny; in short, this democracy, as it has always been taught in theory but from which one has ever moved further away in practice, is henceforth to be regarded as just another utopian fantasy that has bamboozled peoples for so long in order to better enslave and despoil them.

The death of such a system, therefore, is no cause for sadness, but rather a reason for rejoicing. There is always place for rejoicing when a deception is exposed and one is freed of it. Of course, we are leaving this utopian fantasy of parliamentary democracy for a system that is still worse: the ultimate pseudo-democratic state, with its administrative and fiscal tyranny, and its complete enslavement of the masses at the profit of the privileged classes. But waking up from the democratic dream will also perhaps enable us to escape the nightmare that is destined to succeed it.

All empires fall sooner or later. Any political system that denies natural law and only establishes itself by force or constraint, however well-disguised this constraint might be, ends up dashing itself against human reality.

The crystallization of global politics around a few monster totalitarian states will perhaps not even succeed in happening; if it does, however, it likely will not last for long. Many indicators appear to agree that Western civilization is dying out, at least as we have known it from its period of decline since the French Revolution, and certainly since the end of the First World War. Democracy is largely responsible for this. Just as a living organism becomes more vulnerable and contracts illnesses when its immune system weakens, Western societies weakened by materialism, relativism, and other vices of the democratic ideology are also subject to all kinds of attacks.

Immigration from outside of Europe would be one possible reason for the fall of European civilization and of the Western democratic world in general. But there are other potential causes: the collapse of the welfare state; the crash of the banking system and hyperinflation; the depletion of energy resources, especially oil, due either to natural depletion or to war with countries in the Arab world; and finally, world war, the specter of which seems to be hovering more closely as of late. Any one of these trials alone would suffice to plunge the Western world and other parts of the globe into chaos. A combination of several of these things would be fatal.

These are all evils caused by man—this is not a matter of natural catastrophes which could also arise and only serve to aggravate the situation. These are causes for a collapse that the irresponsibility and venality of democratic rulers have allowed to accumulate without seeking any remedies for them. And this accumulation has been produced because democratic states are at the service of the money powers, which have always favored immediate profits in the short term at the expense of the common good and concern for future generations. The moment will come when these unresolved problems will crush societies under them. This will mark a return to reality.

Faced with the threat of such chaos, the Western world is completely powerless. No one in the West is prepared to live without state assistance, paper money, electricity, oil, running water, heat, or electronic devices, and still less within the context of a local or world war, an ethnic cleansing, or a nuclear disaster. Those who survive all of this will have to relearn the basic instincts of social life—things such as solidarity, authority, and loyalty—and the very first gimcrack contrivance of the decadent Western world they will toss aside, almost without even thinking about it, will be parliamentary democracy.

ABOUT THE AUTHOR

Christophe Buffin de Chosal is a Belgian historian and a writer. He is married and the father of six children. He lives in Belgium.

He has worked for 25 years as a high school and university teacher in the fields of History, Economics and Politics. His main fields of expertise are Medieval and Modern History, Modern and Contemporary Politics. Since 1988, he has written articles for *Correspondance européenne*, a French-speaking press agency based in Rome.

In addition to numerous articles in Belgian and international newspapers, Christophe Buffin de Chosal has written two novels and three essays: *Une nouvelle Belgique est-elle possible?* (2009), *Les vraies raisons pour lesquelles les églises se vident* (2012), and *La fin de la démocratie* (2014). The latter book attracted significant attention from French-speaking readers in both Belgium and France.

Made in the USA
San Bernardino, CA
03 October 2017